A WONDERING JEW

Brester School
with good wishes

[signature]

Feb. 2017

A WONDERING JEW

JOHN FIELDSEND

Radec Press

First published May 2014
Reprinted January 2015, August 2015
and April 2016

Radec Press
Email: radecpress@gmail.com

ISBN 978-0-9929094-1-3

Design and layout by
Andrew Harvey
Eayden Press
eaydenpress@yahoo.co.uk

Preface

God saw all that he had made, and it was very good.

Genesis 1:31

The LORD regretted that he had made human beings on the earth, and his heart was deeply troubled.

Genesis 6:6

These scriptures show something of the tension there is in the heart of God, and in the following pages I have tried to share how, in a very small way, I have known something of that tension in my own life experiences. Writing this book has been, on the whole, a positive experience, as it has meant spending several years mulling over the highs and lows of my life, and just to pause and remember has been worthwhile. The main body of the book has been relatively straightforward to write, but when I came to the end of chapter 23 I just did not know how to finish. For many months the text remained uncompleted on the disk of my computer. In the end the last few paragraphs came quickly and unexpectedly; but they comprise some of the most challenging things I have ever experienced or written.

I have had the privilege of sharing my story with thousands of students and others. I say here what I always say to them: 'I have not enjoyed telling you some parts of my story and probably you have not enjoyed listening to all of it. The reason I have told you is that my generation has made such a mess of God's wonderful creation. We are now handing it over to your care; please, please, please make a better job of it than we have done.'

I heard a loud voice from the throne saying, "Look! God's dwelling-place is now among the people, and he will dwell with them. They will be his people, and God himself will be with them and be their God. He will wipe every tear from their eyes. There will be no more death or mourning or crying or pain, for the old order of things has passed away."

He who was seated on the throne said, "I am making everything new!" Then he said, "Write this down, for these words are trustworthy."

Revelation 21:3–5

Acknowledgments

I have much to be grateful for and so many people to thank. I would like to thank my parents for giving me such a wonderful early childhood when they must have been under enormous pressure; they sheltered me from so much of it and were able to leave me such a beautiful farewell letter before they were taken to their horrendous deaths. I want to thank my foster parents, Les and Vera Cumpsty, and their son John for so lovingly and generously opening their home and their hearts to me, not only in my hour of need but continuing to do so for a quarter of a century.

Most of all I want to thank my wife Elizabeth, my light and my soulmate, who has endured and shared something of my travail while I have spent too many hours at my computer keyboard. Also my thanks go to my children and my grandchildren, who continue to reveal to me the wonder and beauty of God's creation reflected in their own lives.

Of course I also thank Sir Nicholas Winton for so generously giving his unstinting commitment in helping to rescue me and another 668 Jewish children from Czechoslovkia when any hope of deliverance seemed to have gone. My granddaughter Anna put it very succinctly in the film *Nicky's Family* when she said, 'Without Sir Nicholas, Grandpa wouldn't have been here, and neither would Daddy or I have been here. So it is a wonderful thing that he did.'

There are many others, far too many to name personally, who have so wonderfully shared their lives and hence enriched mine with their love. I hope those that remain unnamed will understand if I just mention Michael and Jane Tupper, who, by sharing their lives and their love with me and so many others, were part of the foundation that made the development of the fellowship at Christ Church Bayston Hill a reality.

My thanks go out also to Simon Baynes, who took the time to read several early manuscripts of this book and made many helpful suggestions. Also my thanks go to Jenni Dutton for her proof reading and editing work, and to Andrew Harvey whose technical and artistic expertise has greatly enriched this book. However in the end the buck stops here and I take responsibility for any errors that remain.

Contents

x

CHAPTER 1

Surprise, Surprise

Sunday 28 February 1988 is a date that I shall always remember. It had been a pretty ordinary Sunday and Elizabeth and I were well settled down for a quiet evening when the phone rang.

'Hello, John; it's Jane. Did you watch *That's Life!*?'

'No, Jane, not this evening. Why do you ask?'

'Well, you were on it.'

'What do you mean I was on it? I haven't had any contact with Esther Rantzen or anyone else to do with the programme.'

'John, you know that photo you've got of yourself as a little boy in a lace collar?'

'Yes, I know the one you mean, but what's that got to do with it?'

'Well,' said Jane rather hesitantly. 'They showed it right at the beginning of the programme.'

'How could they?' I replied. 'It's never been out of my possession.'

'But they did,' Jane replied more strongly. 'And it was on your travel permit from Czechoslovakia.'

Up to now I had been thinking that this was some kind of leg pull, but I knew that Jane wouldn't leg pull about this.

'What travel permit?' I replied. 'I don't know anything about a travel permit.'

'I don't really know, John, but the item was all about a man called Nicholas Winton. It seems he brought hundreds of Jewish children to England from Czechoslovakia in 1939 just before the war, and you were among them. That's all I can tell you. But they gave a phone number so that any of the children who may have been watching could phone in. Here it is.'

Having said goodbye to Jane, I put down the phone, then hesitantly picked it up again and dialled the number.

'Hello, this is Esther Rantzen speaking…'

I outlined my conversation with Jane, still unsure what this was all about. But things were to become clearer. Elizabeth and I were invited to BBC Television Centre the following Thursday to meet with the many others who had made contact, and then to participate in a follow-up edition of *That's Life!* the following Sunday, when we would all meet Nicholas.

Meeting with one another was a strange and almost surreal experience. Each of our lives in England for nearly half a century had developed in such different directions that but for our shared story we had very little in common. The fact that I had become an Anglican Minister was a source of deep bewilderment to the group, and not least to Esther, whose warm, teasing address to me from then on was, 'Hey, vicar…'

Just a few members of the group had tried to do some background research but had found out nothing. The story that was about to unfold would be almost beyond belief. Esther gave us the bare bones, then moved about among us, listening as we shared our memories. Then we received some preparation for the following Sunday's programme, when we would meet Nicholas.

My mind went into overdrive as my life flashed before me. Of course I knew that I had come to England with a group of Jewish children that had become known as the Kindertransport. I had clear memories of the journey. I had been given a wonderful home by some lovely foster parents, Les and Vera Cumpsty. I had my memories but I had determined that the past was the past and I would live in the present and enjoy the future. So what was this all about? I tried to prepare myself for the Sunday meeting, which would be so personal and emotional for all of us, and yet would be publicly played out on television screens in one of the BBC's most-watched programmes.

Then suddenly, late on Friday evening, the phone rang.

Hello, John, this is Esther. I'd like your advice on a problem. Nicholas has been enlarging upon the way, in 1939, he went about booking trains and gathering the names of Jewish children whose parents wanted him to bring them to the UK. Through the spring and summer of 1939 he managed to transport 669 of the 1000 children the British Government had allowed him to bring. The remaining 331 (his largest transport) were actually on a train in a station in Prague on 3 September, just about to leave, when a message came over the loudspeaker that Britain had joined the war and the train could not leave. The children were taken off the train by the Nazis and none was ever seen again. The renewed memory of this event was so playing on Nicholas's mind that he was actually feeling some responsibility for their fate. What could I say to him?

● IDENTIFICATION CARD

THIS CARD IS ISSUED BY THE BRITISH COMMITTEE FOR CHILDREN IN PRAGUE AND CERTIFIES, THAT ALL PREPARATIONS ACCORDING TO HOME OFFICE RE-QUIREMENTS HAVE BEEN MADE IN ENGLAND FOR THE ADMISSION OF

FEIGE *Hans Heinrich*

WHOSE PHOTOGRAPH IS ATTACHED.

● IDENTITÄTSKARTE

DIESE KARTE IST VOM BRITISH COMMITTEE FOR CHILDREN IN PRAG AUSGESTELLT UND BEGLAUBIGT, DASS ALLE VORBEREITUNGEN ÜBEREINSTIMMEND MIT DEN HOME OFFICE BESTIMMUNGEN IN ENGLAND ZUR EINREISEBEWILLIGUNG FÜR

FEIGE *Hans Heinrich*

GEMACHT WURDEN, DESSEN FOTOGRAFIE ANGEBRACHT IST.

NAME	DATE OF BIRTH	PLACE OF BIRTH
H.FEIGE *Hans Heinrich*	14.IX.1931	Troppau

PARENTS NAMES
Curt
Gertrud } FEIGE

ADDRESS
Weigstadtl
Ostsudetengau
Kirchengasse 40

BRITISH COMMITTEE FOR CHILDREN IN PRAGUE.

000115

● IDENTIFICATION CARD

THIS CARD IS ISSUED BY THE BRITISH COMMITTEE FOR CHILDREN IN PRAGUE AND CERTIFIES, THAT ALL PREPARATIONS ACCORDING TO HOME OFFICE RE-QUIREMENTS HAVE BEEN MADE IN ENGLAND FOR THE ADMISSION OF

FEIGE *Hans Heinrich*

WHOSE PHOTOGRAPH IS ATTACHED.

● IDENTITÄTSKARTE

DIESE KARTE IST VOM BRITISH COMMITTEE FOR CHILDREN IN PRAG AUSGESTELLT UND BEGLAUBIGT, DASS ALLE VORBEREITUNGEN ÜBEREINSTIMMEND MIT DEN HOME OFFICE BESTIMMUNGEN IN ENGLAND ZUR EINREISEBEWILLIGUNG FÜR

FEIGE *Hans Heinrich*

GEMACHT WURDEN, DESSEN FOTOGRAFIE ANGEBRACHT IST.

NAME	DATE OF BIRTH	PLACE OF BIRTH
FEIGE *Hans Heinrich*	11.IX.1931	Troppau

PARENTS NAMES
Curt
Gertrud } FEIGE

ADDRESS
Weigstadtl
Ostsudetengau
Kirchengasse 40

BRITISH COMMITTEE FOR CHILDREN IN PRAGUE.

000115

THIS PART TO BE DETACHED AND SENT TO THE ALIENS DEPARTMENT HOME OFFICE.

My travel document.

Off the top of my head I made some tentative suggestions to which Esther replied, 'Thanks, John: you've just got yourself a job. You say it to him.'

It was not easy in just a few words and before a studio and nationwide audience to speak to the pain of a person's totally undeserved sense of guilt. I did what I could and hopefully gave Nicholas some peace of mind. Esther then referred to my travel document, with which the previous Sunday's programme had begun. This document was part of a host of papers that Nicholas had stashed away in the loft of his house and forgotten about. 'Would you like to give this to John?' she suggested, to which Nicholas generously agreed. This made me raise some serious questions. Why did Nicholas still have this document in his possession? Surely it should have been handed in to the immigration officers when I first arrived in the UK. In response Nicholas explained that at the time the British Home Office was sometimes rather slow in providing the necessary paperwork; they did not always seem to appreciate the urgency of the situation.

'So what could I do?' he said. 'I set up a small printing press and started to print my own.'

This left me with another question: 'Could this make me an illegal immigrant?'

'No,' Nicholas replied to my relief. 'By the time I got the children to England I had always got the real papers. I only used my forgeries to get the children through Germany. Your real papers will be somewhere in the Home Office vaults, if they have kept them.'

With that I relaxed. Now Nicholas's forged document has become one of my most valued possessions.

CHAPTER 2

How Could it Have Happened?

Over the years prior to *That's Life!* other events had conspired to raise childhood memories, but this was different; it was more dynamic, and it demanded a more active response. It aroused in me a deep desire not only to research my own past, my own journey, but also to try my utmost to discover what had happened to my parents and to the rest of my family. But foundational to this was my need to discover and try to understand how it was possible for the Holocaust to have happened at all in one of the most highly civilised countries and advanced cultures the world had yet known. How could this have been possible? Were the German people by upbringing and conviction systemically anti-Semitic? This did not fit in with my experience of the Germans I had met in a variety of contexts in the increasingly complex global village that this world was rapidly becoming.

The only way I could allow myself to begin my own personal journey with any kind of integrity would be to do so in the context of investigating and evaluating the wider issues raised by the Holocaust; otherwise I would be in danger of engaging in what could easily degenerate into an over-melodramatic 'poor me' sob story that I wanted to avoid at all costs. It did not feel like that, for despite all that had happened, my experience was that life was good. I had had a secure and happy childhood, albeit dramatically shortened, with my loving parents. My caring foster parents generously shared their home through the difficult years of World War II, and through the challenging times of my teenage rebellion, supporting me right through my education, including eight years at two universities. Now I have a wonderful home with Elizabeth. Together we have given life to three lovely children who themselves have given us seven delightful grandchildren.

So what I shall be sharing, although in one way intensely personal, will also be broadly representative of the many experiences of the 10,000 other Kindertransport children – though for some their experiences may not have been as wholly positive as mine. But I am also preparing to tell my story as a tribute to those one and a half million children who did not escape and who died tragic deaths at the hands of the Nazi persecutors. Statistics can sound cold and impersonal, but for me at least they come to life when I sit in the beautifully awesome Children's Memorial at Yad Vashem in Jerusalem, listening to the roll-call of their names. Seeing a candlelight for each child leads me to contemplate the thought that I missed my name being there by about five weeks, through the courage and foresight of one young businessman from Hampstead, and through one family's generosity in sharing their home with me.

My interest in trying to understand the rise of Nazism led me to look at the Paris Peace Conference of 1919–20, which took place at Versailles. A key product of the conference was the Versailles

Treaty, in which the amount of disarmament, reparations and territorial changes to be imposed on Germany was agreed. The conference also saw the establishment of the League of Nations, through which it was intended that any future international conflicts would be resolved peacefully. The demands made upon Germany were indeed heavy, especially regarding financial compensation and the dismantling of its industrial manufacturing capability. This caused rampant inflation and the rapid disintegration of German life and culture. Just to give some examples of how quickly this affected everyday life in Germany, in 1919 the exchange rate was twelve German Marks to one US dollar. By December 1922 this had risen to 7000 Marks to a US dollar, and by the end of 1923 the Mark was almost valueless. In 1921 a five Mark stamp could be used to post a letter in Germany, but by 1923 this had risen to 50 million Marks. It has been well argued that these harsh results of the Versailles Treaty, compounded by a series of weak German governments, opened the way for the rise of Nazism and the appointment of Adolf Hitler as the German Chancellor. None of this, of course, excuses Hitler's innate anti-Semitism, which is clearly described in his well-known book *Mein Kampf*. In this book he describes how his thinking developed from having little knowledge of anything Jewish to developing a political anti-Semitism to a thoroughgoing systemic anti-Semitism based on what he considered to be a revelatory religious understanding: 'Thus I believe today that I am acting according to the will of the Almighty Creator: *when I defend myself against the Jew, I am fighting for the work of the Lord*' (italics mine).

In a nation undergoing a complex crisis, which was not only financial and political but deeply challenging to its confidence in its own nationhood, Hitler's thesis had an increasing appeal to the German intelligentsia. With its theological dimension it also attracted support from many sections of the Church in Germany, both Roman Catholic and Protestant. The subtle argument, which had such appeal, was this: Germany's defeat in the war was not caused by military superiority of the victorious Allies but by Jewish degenerative influences from within. Similarly its financial and industrial weakness was not the result of the Versailles Treaty but of the greed of the major Jewish influence in Germany's financial and industrial structures. And as far as Germany's own dented self-image was concerned, this was due to the weakening purity of the Aryan super-race by intermingling with Jewish blood. As well as identifying convincing scapegoats within Germany this philosophy had two further advantages for Hitler's plans. First it could be used to persuade the victorious Allies that Germany did not hold them as primarily responsible for its defeat and downfall, and secondly, it further encouraged those in the rest of the world who were susceptible to anti-Semitic thinking to blame world Jewry for the economic crash it was experiencing in the 1930s. The first of these resulted in the United States, which in any case had not been very supportive of the Versailles Treaty, making generous loans to support the German economy in the late 1920s. However when the USA began to experience the worldwide crash of the early thirties it demanded its loans be repaid, meaning any hope of Germany's resurrection seemed doomed. Germany's weak government was unable to offer any way forward, and in 1933 Hitler's Nazi Party, which thus far had made no real impact on the German political scene, was swept to power. I believe it was a vote of desperation rather than of real political or personal conviction. This was the last-ditch stand of a people without hope.

Why did I research all this and in what way did it help me in my personal search? In no way did it cause me to make any excuses for Hitler's evil intent and action. However it helped me to deal with any latent anti-German attitudes deep in my own heart, so that I could develop my proposed family searches without any residual, generalised anti-German feelings. From this point my research would further my own inner healing rather than deepen any unresolved bitterness. In no way could I support what Germany had done, but at least I could begin to understand how it had come about.

CHAPTER 3

All Change

Sometime in the mid-1920s my mother, Trude Steiner, left her home in the little town of Vitkov, near Opava, in the newly created Republic of Czechoslovakia. She intended to study photography in Dresden in Saxon Germany, because Dresden

Mother as a student.

was one of the main European centres for that subject. There she met my father, a young German businessman named Curt Feige, who was a fashion buyer for one of Dresden's department stores. They married and settled in a new flat in Gruna, a newly developing district of Dresden, just east of the Volkspark Grosse Garten, which contained Dresden Zoo. My father's parents, Fritz and Betty, and his brother Alfred lived nearby, as did his sister Erna, who had married a man called Moritz Weiler. Erna and Moritz had three children, Edith, Horst (later Harry) and Gerda. Alfred was not married. I do not remember much about my father's side of the family, partly because I was still young when we left Dresden, but also, as I was to learn much later from my Uncle Alfred, there was some kind of rift between my father

Father, mother and Arthur.

With our lovely car.

and the rest of the family. The nature of this rift will always remain unknown.

Despite the very difficult economic situation, at first life seemed full of promise, especially as the possibility of American financial support dawned like a new light on the horizon. Curt and Trude's first son, Gert Arthur, was born in March 1928. Though not fully practising Jews, Curt and Trude were members of a nearby Liberal Synagogue. A growing cloud of anti-Semitism, fuelled by Hitler's Nazi Party, was beginning to affect the atmosphere in some of Germany's cities, not least Dresden, but Curt was not overly concerned. After all, he had been awarded the Iron Cross, Germany's highest military medal, during World War I, and Curt felt that this would give him security if any problems arose. So life was good. My parents were among the up-and-coming middle-class couples who could afford to live in a pleasant area and run a good car (which of course my father needed for his work as a buyer). They could also afford regular holidays with my mother's family in Vitkov. But this way of life was not to last long. Following on from the Wall Street Crash and America's demands for repayment of its loans, Germany entered another period of severe economic and political instability. One outcome of this was the rapid growth and deepening influence of the Communist Party on the extreme left and Hitler's National Socialist German Workers Party, known as the Nazi Party, on the extreme right. This led to the outbreak of riots between supporters of the two parties, and Dresden was one of the cities deeply affected by this. Ironically, in *Mein Kampf* Hitler demonstrated that he understood the Jews to be very much in the Communist camp while the Communists saw the Jews as very much involved in German capitalism. At this time in 1931 Trude and Curt Feige were expecting their second child (me), so Trude returned to her parents' home in Czechoslovakia for a secure and safe delivery, and this is where I was born. Shortly after my birth, my mother brought me home to Dresden, where my father and my elder brother were waiting. These were not easy years and the increasing instability finally led to President Hindenburg appointing Hitler as Chancellor of Germany in January 1933. Hitler's rise to power is an interesting and important story in itself and is well documented elsewhere.

In short, Hitler's Nazi Party had won increasing influence and power in the late 1920s while in the early years of the 1930s its support was on the wane. Had there been full elections it is very much open to question whether Hitler would have had sufficient support. However the ageing, weary President Hindenburg made the last-ditch decision to install him following a series of ineffective previous appointments. In the months following his appointment, Hitler set about his work by using Article 48 of the Weimar constitution to make himself absolute ruler. His real intentions became clear when in March 1933 he orchestrated anti-Semitic riots in Berlin. In May there followed the public burning of Jewish books and by October all Berlin hospitals had been 'cleansed' of Jewish doctors. What happened in Berlin was speedily replicated in other cities, and in Dresden these policies were particularly effectively worked out.

In the midst of all this my parents maintained a stable, loving home and I am privileged to have many family photographs of those early years. How those photographs came into my possession will be a topic in a later chapter. My parents made those times as normal as possible in very difficult circumstances and we frequently went to my grandparents' home in Vitkov for holidays in summer and in winter. From my pictures I can tell that the sun was always shining in summer and there was always plenty of snow in winter.

*First day at school
in Dresden.*

I started school in Dresden in 1935. As the photo shows, I am looking pretty pleased with myself, carrying my *Zuckertüte* (a cone full of sweets given to children in Germany on their first day at school), but shortly after this things began to change rapidly. There was dramatic growth in the Hitler Youth movement, and in 1935 100,000 German youth took an oath of eternal enmity to the Jewish people. Most of the children at school began to come in Hitler Youth uniforms, and Jew-baiting and bullying became the norm of our experience.

The apartment blocks where we lived were in groups of four, surrounding a large quadrangle that included a well-designed play area with sandpits, swings and other equipment. My brother and I regularly played with the many other children from the

17

With Arthur in the sandpit

apartments and had a great time together. However, quite suddenly, the other children started to name-call my brother and me as dirty Jews – and so the bullying began. We were kicked, punched and spat upon. I remember one incident especially vividly. Things had become particularly aggressive, so my brother ran back into our apartment and brought out our father's Iron Cross to try to convince our friends that although we were Jewish, we could still be loyal Germans; but it was to no avail: the bullying continued and even intensified.

Two other incidents when I was about five or six are also deeply etched in my memory. The first was when my father and I were having one of our father–son tickling romps and I hit my head on the sharp edge of one of the apartment's old-fashioned radiators. Of course I started crying so my father tickled me all the more with the result that I hit my head all the harder and it started bleeding from a deep cut in my forehead. Father took me off to our family doctor who took one look at the cut and said, 'That needs stitching,' but then added, 'I don't stitch Jews.' He put on a plaster and I still have a scar to show for it. The second incident showed even more clearly the way things were rapidly changing. I have said we were a Liberal Jewish family. Nowhere was this shown more clearly than the fact that my parents had many non-Jewish friends and felt well integrated into the wider non-Jewish Dresden community. In fact my father's closest friends were Gentiles. Mr and Mrs Schmidt (not their real names) had two boys, the same ages as my brother and me, and our families were very close and spent a lot of time together. So it came as a complete surprise when one day the two Schmidt boys started name-calling and abusing my brother and me. We then realised that Mr Schmidt had joined the SS.

At this point my father saw the dangerous situation we would be in if we remained in Dresden. So late one night, without any goodbyes, we simply got into our car, with only the most basic of our possessions, and drove through the night to my mother's parents' home in Czechoslovakia. Fortunately, because we carried so few possessions, we did not raise any suspicions with the border guards.

CHAPTER 4

Czechoslovakia – A False Dawn

We arrived in Vitkov with a real sense of relief and security. We were now in a free, democratic country and in the bosom of my mother's warm, welcoming family. We were four generations living in a large villa. The villa had been designed for my grandparents by Arnold Karplus, my grandmother's brother, a well-known architect who had been born in Vitkov but was now living and practising in Vienna. I was very close to my great grandfather, described in official records as a businessman, but whom I remember from a photograph of him

Back row, left to right, Trude and Curt Feige, Samuel Steiner
Front row Benedict and Berta Karplus, Rosa Steiner
Bottom right Heini and Arthur Feige.

in uniform as a fireman with a horse-drawn fire engine. Maybe he had formed his own fire-fighting company! My brother was closest to our grandfather, Dr Samuel Steiner, whose profession he would one day follow, but in very different circumstances and in a different land.

But our new situation was not to last. A series of dramatic changes were to follow, which first altered our circumstances and then revolutionised our lives. Shortly after our arrival, my great grandparents, Benedict and Berta Karplus, moved into a Jewish care home for the elderly in Opava. Then my grandparents, Samuel and Rosa Steiner, moved to Prague. This left us once more as a nuclear family. However we had made good friends. My brother Arthur and I attended the local school, and there was a small family-run carpentry workshop just down the lane from our house where we spent hours making things from off-cuts of timber. Also the house next to ours was the Roman Catholic Presbytery where there lived a very friendly priest. Vitkov was in Czech Sudetenland (German for 'southern lands'), formerly West Silesia. The area was bilingual, Czech and German being equally favoured, so we had no language problems as a German-speaking family.

But by now nationalistic tensions were beginning to increase. Czechoslovakia had been established in 1920 by the League of Nations and was the newest and one of the best-run democracies of the new Europe. Yet although it was 'new' in terms of its newly established boundaries and form of government, its various parts had long and distinguished histories. For instance the foundation of Prague University predates that of both Oxford and Cambridge Universities. Prague's Old-New Synagogue, established in 1270, is the oldest active synagogue in Europe. Many of the Czech cities can trace their foundations back to very early times, and Opava, the town where I was born, was established in the twelfth century as a thriving merchant town. One thing that comes out very clearly is that Jewish communities were well established in the Czech lands and often, though not always, experienced a freedom they did not usually experience in other parts of Europe.

By reason of its geographic situation right in the heart of Europe, Czechoslovakia's population was fairly cosmopolitan, including Slavs in the east and Germans in the north. There was a fairly significant population of German origin in Sudetenland, along Czechoslovakia's northern border with Germany. Many (perhaps the majority) in this group were very open to identifying with the new Czechoslovakia after World War I, but then began to identify more closely with their German roots as Hitler gained increasing power in his homeland. The same could be said of the Austro–Czech communities in the south and the east of the land. The reason that these communities existed becomes clear when it is seen that Czechoslovakia was carved out of what had been the Austro-Hungarian Empire in which Germany had had major involvement.

In order to understand how these groups manifested themselves we have to return to the Versailles Treaty. One of its stipulations was the demilitarisation and Allied control of large sections of the Rhineland area of Germany until 1935. However, as a goodwill gesture to the new German Weimar Republic, the last Allied troops had left in 1930. During these between-war years Hitler was strongly rearming Germany at a rate totally in contravention of the Treaty, but the Allies took no action to stop this. On 7 March 1936 Hitler moved German troops into the Rhineland and effectively took military control there. This led to some considerable concern among the Allied political leadership but Hitler developed a two-pronged foreign policy that effectively calmed this concern. The first prong was to reassure the Allies that his only territorial aims were to regain some of the land Germany had lost as a result of his defeat in World War I. His second prong, which was probably as effective, was to try to convince the Allies that the real threat to world peace and stability did not come from Germany but from the international Jewish community. In this he had no little success and gained real support in some sections of the British and French leadership.

In 1937 Lord Halifax met with Hitler to express the Allied concern about Germany's disregard of the limitations placed upon it by the Versailles Treaty, especially with respect to its obvious moves to annexe Austria as a part of 'Greater Germany'. Despite these protests the *Anschluss* (union) took place on 13 March 1938 when the German army marched unopposed into Austria. Hitler correctly sensed that the Allied protests in response to his action were muted and half-hearted, and he made clear his demands that Czech Sudetenland be handed over to Germany. On 29 September 1938 the British Prime Minister, Neville Chamberlain, met with Hitler in Munich and, in the absence of any Czech representation, agreed to Hitler's demands, following his assurances that this would conclude Germany's expansionist plans.

Chamberlain landed at Heston Aerodrome on 30 September 1938, and spoke to the crowds there:

The settlement of the Czechoslovakian problem, which has now been achieved is, in my view, only the prelude to a larger settlement in which all Europe may find peace. This morning I had another talk with the German Chancellor, Herr Hitler, and here is the paper which bears his name upon it as well as mine. Some of you, perhaps, have already heard what it contains but I would just like to read it to you: '... We regard the agreement signed last night and the Anglo–German Naval Agreement as symbolic of the desire of our two peoples never to go to war with one another again.'

However another part of this agreement was that the Czech Government should be persuaded to cede Sudetenland to Germany without any Czech resistance, so the Czech Government was informed that if it resisted the accession of the Sudetenland territory it would not receive any Allied support.

So far all the discussions about Hitler have related to Nazi threats to the wider European nations. To look more directly at Hitler's plans vis-a-vis the Jewish people we have to backtrack a few months to an international conference that President Roosevelt of the USA convened at Evian-les-Bains in France in July 1938. The agenda was to discuss the issue of increasing numbers of Jewish refugees seeking to flee from Nazi persecution. For eight days representatives from 32 countries and 39 private organisations, together with twenty-four voluntary bodies, met to consider the implications for immigration quotas. So far Great Britain had made the most generous provisions, but the international consensus was that no increase in already-set quotas could be considered. The only country willing to further open its borders was the Dominican Republic of Central America. The Nazis realised that their destructive anti-Semitic plans would not evoke any great international reaction.

Our little town of Vitkov, which had been relatively free from these racial and religious tensions, now became embroiled in this new situation. Although I was still very young I was becoming aware of increasing pressure on my parents. I particularly remember one time, I think it may have been my seventh birthday, when I didn't receive a present that I had set my heart on. Fighting back the tears of disappointment, I thought to myself, 'My parents are under great stress; I mustn't add to it.'

That my feelings were not misplaced became clear when one day the German army – tanks, cavalry and infantry – invaded our town and took control of it. I have two very clear memories of this time. First the German soldiers confiscated our car, which my parents had cared for so carefully, and used it as a kind of dodgem or stock car – something to charge around in just for the fun of it. This must have hurt my parents grievously. My second memory (and it is strange what we remember), was when I was helping (or hindering) my father who was cutting down a diseased plum tree (yes, I'm sure it was a plum tree, not that that's relevant to the story). As we were working we became aware of heavy footsteps and a jack-booted, black-shirted SS officer approaching us up the garden path. For no other reason except a bit of Jew-baiting the questioning began: 'Why are you cutting down that tree?' And at the blink of an eye the simple act of cutting down a diseased tree turned into a frightening SS interrogation. It is something that I will remember for the rest of my life.

Not long after this my father called Arthur and me to come into the living room. 'Sit down,' he said. 'I have something very important to tell you. You are going on a long journey. You are to travel to a country called England. You will have to go alone; we can't come with you. Maybe one day, when the present troubles are over, you will be able to return, or maybe we can join you, but for now you will have to go alone.' Then he taught me to say these few important words: 'I can't speak English.' (Arthur on the other hand did have a smattering of the language.)

The last photo before going to the station.

A few days later my mother took a last photograph of father, Arthur and me. They then took us to our little local railway station, put us on a train and we quietly said our goodbyes. Then, as the train began to move, my mother took off her wristwatch and passed it to me, saying, 'This is for you to remember us by.' The next part of the journey is something of a blur in my memory. How long the journey was and who, if anyone, travelled with us I shall never know. My next clear memory is arriving at a Jewish boarding school, the *Israelitische Gartenbauschule*, at Ahlem on the outskirts of Hanover, back in Germany. Just how long we remained there I cannot say, but it was anything from a few weeks to a couple of months. Nor shall I ever know why we had gone there. Of the schooling I have no memories except that the regime was strict. Every

Morning exercises at the Gartenbouschule.

morning we were awakened with the march from *Aida* coming over the loudspeakers, and our first activity was PE on a large quad before breakfast. Another memory is that I made a special friendship with one other boy who was about to leave on the next part of his journey. Without thinking how it might be possible, we wanted to keep in touch, so we planned to write each other's names on bits of paper. But even this piece of childlike innocence was not without its problems. We were making this pact of friendship on the Sabbath, and writing was considered to be work, so we hid behind a bush to fulfil our agreement, but a prefect had seen us and did much more work on our backsides than we had done on the paper.

From there things moved rapidly and so disjointedly that I cannot really give a coherent account. One day just Arthur and I were taken to Hanover railway station and put on a train, which was already well filled with other children and a very few adults. We travelled on through Germany in a silent mood of fear as there were also some Nazi guards on board. We then came to an international border, which turned out to be with Holland. The Nazi guards got off, some much more friendly adults got on and we travelled on to a place where we got onto a boat. By then it was dark and we were tired so I have only blurred memories. However of the next morning I have clear memories. We were on what seemed to me to be a very large ship on a great expanse of water. The only other ships I had ever seen were the paddle-steamers on the River Elbe in Dresden. Shortly we docked in a harbour, which I later knew was Harwich. I remember seeing quite a lot of other boats, including a grey one with lots of guns. Also there was a big aeroplane with four engines, floating on the water. All this was totally new and exciting to me, so exciting that I began to forget my fears. We were then put on another train and taken to a big station in a big city. We had arrived at Liverpool Street station in London.

CHAPTER 5

In a New Country

The station platform was alive with hundreds of children with labels round our necks, jabbering away in Czech and German. There were groups of adults not understanding a word and looking at the labels for particular names and numbers, and there were a few organisers trying to keep some sense of order. Eventually Arthur and I were found by a lady whom I would learn to call Aunty Vera. After a few formalities we were taken into the street outside the station in order to board a bus. I shall always remember my sense of sheer terror at the double-decker, never having seen one before, which I was completely convinced would turn over! Young as I was I was already developing an interest in mechanical transport. At home my favourite toy had been Trix, something akin to Meccano, and I had always been interested in models of various forms of transport. I well remember a time, a few months after coming to England, when I was asked what I wanted to be. I replied, 'I'm going to be a doctor to a motor car.'

The three of us spent the night somewhere in London, and the next day took a train to Sheffield, where Aunty Vera lived. We took a tram (again a double-decker) to the house, where we were met by our new 'uncle', Les. Here I was to come face to face with my next object of terror – an open fire! 'Help, the house is

Les and Vera Cumpsty with their son John.

burning down!' was my immediate reaction. After some reassurance I settled down and started to come to terms with my new surroundings. I was very grateful that Arthur was still with me. He had been scheduled to go to another foster family, but for various reasons they were not ready to take him, so Les and Vera offered to let him to stay for a while. It certainly helped me and was probably a help all round. Also I had a new 'brother', Aunty Vera and Uncle Les's son John, who was very welcoming, as was their lovely mixed-breed terrier dog. John was just seven months older than me and we were to become very good and close friends.

Memories of the rest of the day are fairly grey and unremarkable until bedtime. Our new home in Handsworth, a southern suburb of Sheffield, was a typical small semi-detached house on a typical northern estate, so, with the extra, unexpected new arrival we had to be three in a double bed – but that was not my real problem. My real problem was sheets and blankets. Where, in this multi-layered complex, did one get in? I had only ever slept under a continental quilt!

After the shocks of double-decker transport, open fires and sheets and blankets, we quickly settled in and were made to feel very welcome and very much at home. One decision that urgently had to be made was how we should be named. At home we had always been called by our second names, so for my brother it was simple: he could remain Arthur, and so Gert Arthur became Gerald Arthur. For me also the decision was obvious. My second name of Heinrich (or Heini as I was usually called) simply translated to Henry, and my first name of Hans became John, as is usual. However, for reasons that will become clear in a later chapter, after answering to Henry for many years, I eventually made the decision to be called John.

The other children around us were so friendly that the pain of our past experiences began to fade. It was amazing how we learnt to get along even with our limited language. I didn't have to use my 'I can't speak English' phrase very often. It was now mid-July in the beautiful summer of 1939. The schools were soon to break up for the long summer holidays. There was a very large wood at the bottom of our garden which we roamed and played in for hours on end, so life took on a new happiness.

Also we were able still to correspond with our parents, somehow hoping that our separation could be resolved sooner rather than later. Most importantly we were able to send some photographs in order to reassure our parents that we had safely arrived at a good home and were being happily cared for.

There was one other new thing in our lives that would eventually bring a fundamental change. Our new family was deeply Christian and went to church every Sunday. Les, in fact, was the leader of the Sunday school. There was no pressure upon us to conform, but there was no way Les and Vera could leave two young children at home in a foreign land while they went to church. Naturally we went with them, and we enjoyed the experience.

But one thing foreshadowed what might yet come to pass. Uncle Les was so convinced there would be a war that as early as January 1939 he had begun to build an air-raid shelter in the garden. It was underground, bomb-proof against anything but a direct hit and gas-proof (it would later be voted the best air-raid shelter in Sheffield), but of course I did not understand any of these things at the time. All I remember is the neighbours looking over the fence and laughing at Uncle Les, saying, 'What are you doing? There isn't going to be a war!' With hindsight I realise that Noah must have experienced something like this when he was building his ark!

I recall one other very clear memory of those early experiences of life in a new country and that is of a very happy holiday in Bridlington. It was my first experience of a glorious seaside. As I remember it the sun never ceased to shine, the sea was always warm and calm, and the endless beach was a wonderful place for building sandcastles and playing all manner of games. But once more things were about to change.

CHAPTER 6

The War Begins

On 3 September 1939 we were all at home in Sheffield. There was an atmosphere of foreboding in the room. We all fell silent as the radio was switched on. I felt the silence but did not really understand what this was all about. The voice of the British Prime Minister, Neville Chamberlain, cut through the silence:

I am speaking to you from the Cabinet Room at 10 Downing Street. This morning the British Ambassador in Berlin handed the German Government a final note stating that, unless we hear from them by 11 o'clock that they were prepared at once to withdraw their troops from Poland, a state of war would exist between us. I have to tell you now that no such undertaking has been received, and that consequently this country is at war with Germany.

The Prime Minister continued for some while, outlining the background to this decision and how things might develop. I can't pretend to have understood the full significance of what was happening, but I picked up the emotions and realised that our brief good times had come to an end. Looking back, one of the things that continues to amaze me is that within the space of about nine weeks I had learned sufficient English to absorb the basic meaning of what I was hearing.

During that night the air-raid sirens wailed across Sheffield. There was no attack. It may have been a practice or a false alarm, but this I remember. We got out of bed, put on some outer garments and dashed down to that wonderful air-raid shelter. But to our consternation we could hardly get in. Our neighbours had got there first! For the next few weeks all was quiet as we entered the 'phony war' stage.

My entry into English school life that September has also left some memories. After all it was my third school in three countries in as many years. I had been in England only about ten weeks and yet I do not remember ever needing to say, 'I can't speak English.' A group of us children from our area of Sheffield went to a school on Prince of Wales Road, which entailed a lovely mile-long walk through the large wood near our house. However one day we left it a bit late so we took a shortcut over some iron railings onto the main road; at least all the other children climbed over but I tried to go through. I pushed my head through but that was all, and in the end I had to be extricated by the Sheffield Fire Brigade!

For a while life seemed to be settling down again, but it was not to last. We regularly listened to a radio transmission by William Joyce (or Lord Haw Haw as he was popularly known). Joyce, who was born in the USA, raised in Ireland and now living in Germany, used to broadcast threats from Germany intended to create fear among the British population. However on the whole he was received with some amusement by his British listeners. The German Luftwaffe had for a while been intending to bomb the industrial centre of Sheffield, but so far the British defences had successfully interfered with the Luftwaffe radio-navigation system. I remember one day Lord Haw Haw saying that even if Sheffield were put on wheels they would find it. We thought this slightly comical, but it turned out that the German scientists had found some way through the defence system and, on the nights of 12 and 15 December 1940, Sheffield was heavily blitzed. This meant that for a time all Sheffield schools were closed and we had lessons in small groups in various homes.

When we went back to school, I did not return to the school on Prince of Wales Road, but instead started at a school on Handsworth Road, for no other reason than adjustments to catchment areas. So in the space of 18 months or so I notched up three schools. After this Uncle Les was promoted from Under-Manager at Tinsley Park Colliery to Inspector of Mines and Quarries for Nottinghamshire, Derbyshire and South Yorkshire. This meant a move to Worksop, and in order to facilitate this I went to live with Vera's sister Ruby and her husband Martin in Renhold, near Bedford, for a few months – hence one more school on my tally. Vera's sister and her husband did not have any children of their own, but they had already opened their home to an evacuee from London. Bedford was not the quietest place for evacuation, however, and again we spent many nights in an air-raid shelter. My new 'uncle', Martin, was, like my father, in the clothing industry, but now instead of fashion it was uniforms and parachute material. I remember a trip with Uncle Martin to Coventry. As it was just after the horrendous Blitz, many of the shop shells were still smouldering, and whilst standing in front of a bombed ladies outfitters, it took me a while to realise that the 'bodies' in the wrecked shop windows were mannequins, not real people.

During the following years I also spent part of the long summer holidays with Aunty Vera's sister Edna and her husband, Bob. Bob had been a successful farmer in Grafton Underwood, but his farm had been requisitioned to become a bomber station for US B19 Flying Fortresses, and as part compensation he had been given a redundant farmhouse and smallholding nearby. I remember seeing the shot-up planes returning after their costly daylight bombing raids. Many were so damaged that we could see daylight through their shattered wings and fuselages. Some sent out signal flares of various colours, indicating that their radios had failed and they were requesting priority landing slots, either because they were in danger of crashing or had severely injured aircrew on-board.

Though the war had started my brother and I still received correspondence from our parents, but the German leadership only allowed the use of International Red Cross mail forms, which limited each side to a maximum of 15 words. Eventually even the flow of this correspondence slowed and then ceased, leaving us very much hanging in the air as to what was happening to the families we had left behind.

I returned to Les and Vera after they were settled in Worksop. Instead of a local primary school they sent their own son and me to the prep department of King Edward VI Grammar School in East Retford, so we could later transfer to the main school without further disruption. This was, towards me at any rate, a very generous act, as it involved a certain amount of school fees. In September 1942 I transferred to the main school and felt at last that I would remain settled for a while, not that it was a normal school life even now. A whole school from the east coast (Great Yarmouth, if I remember correctly) had been evacuated to East Retford. They occupied the school buildings from early to mid-morning and again late in the afternoon, and we used them for the middle part of the day, but it worked quite well.

During this time I became aware of phone calls and letters and finally a visit from someone from Bloomsbury House, the offices of the Jewish Refugee Committee (JRC). I was not at any stage directly involved or consulted in what was happening, but I began to sense a change in the air. Eventually Les and Vera told me that the JRC were concerned that I was not getting a proper Jewish education, and they had decided that I should go to Stoatley Rough School, a boarding school in Haslemere, Surrey, mainly for Jewish refugee children.

CHAPTER 7

Stoatley Rough School

First of all I should explain that the school took its name because a 'rough' in that part of Surrey was a plot of land on which a house was built – it had nothing to do with the nature of the school or its pupils! So, in September 1943, at the age of 12, I was about to enter my eighth school.

One day Vera took me to Waterloo station in London where I met up with some of the other children and school staff, most of whom spoke with a strong German accent. It took me straight back to a similar situation at Liverpool Street station just four

With Arthur and John Cumpsty in Sheffield.

years ago, and unearthed many confusing thoughts and memories. However I soon settled in to what was a small, very well-run, liberal coeducational boarding school in several acres of beautiful grounds.

The main house had once been a large private residence and now comprised the teaching areas, domestic and dining facilities, plus dormitories for the younger pupils. There was hutted accommodation for the middle years and finally there was accommodation for the more senior pupils on a small farm attached to the school. Also on the farm site was a small, unheated open-air swimming pool. The school was run on the basis of mutual respect and self-discipline, with a minimum of rules, so outside the set pattern of lessons, mealtimes, bedtime and other timetabled activities we were free to roam the whole area (which included the lovely spots of Hindhead Heath, Gibbet Hill and the Devil's Punchbowl) as much as we wished.

Most of us went home for normal school holidays, though there was a nucleus of refugee children for whom this was their permanent home. During my three years at the school my foster mother had to have extended periods of surgery and recuperation, and I therefore spent some holidays at the school. During one of these times a group of us boys collected several hundred yards of old telephone cable that had been left on Hindhead Heath by the Army, which had previously used the area for training exercises. With this cable and a few other accessories we built our own somewhat basic but workable telephone link between the hutted and the farm accommodation. The school had good games and sports facilities as the teacher in charge of this had been a member of the German Olympic team, but had been banned from competing in the 1936 Berlin Olympics because he was Jewish. The school curriculum was, on the whole, well taught, although one serious limitation was that there were no laboratories, meaning science teaching was almost nonexistent. Many of the staff were non-resident, including the vicar of Haslemere, who taught Geography.

Shortly after the end of the war in Europe on 8 May 1945, we were joined by three new pupils. One was a boy from Holland and the other two, a brother and sister, were from Poland. The siblings had survived the war by hiding down the sewers of Warsaw. All three were a great addition to our close school community, and the boy from Holland became one of my special friends. On 8 June the following year, after the defeat of Japan, the two of us were given special permission to catch an early train to London to be at the big victory celebrations.

But I also recall what was, for my brother and me, an even more memorable event, though I cannot now put a date on it. Without any expectation we received a large parcel from Czechoslovakia under the auspices of the International Red Cross. On opening we were overjoyed to find our three family photograph albums. How they came into the hands of the Red Cross we shall never know, but they are a wonderful treasure and a reassurance that the memories of our early life are accurate, and not the product of over-stimulated imaginations. To our great joy we saw on the final pages of the last album some of the photos we had been able to send after our arrival in England. What a blessing these pictures must have been.

With the stresses of the war over some of the aspects of our Jewish upbringing, which had been somewhat neglected, were tightened up, and Bar Mitzvah preparation classes were established at school, led by a small but growing Jewish community in Hindhead. As these classes progressed I became aware of an increasing conflict in my own thinking over what I really believed, and so, just before my Bar Mitzvah, which was due at the end of the summer term in 1946, I asked for a postponement so I could have time to think. While at home for the long summer holidays the JRC arranged a meeting for me with a rabbi in Sheffield. However, when I arrived at his house and was greeted by his wife, it transpired that he had forgotten to look at his diary and had gone out for the day on other business. I wrote back to the JRC asking them to rearrange the meeting. Instead they replied that the matter was now over, and I should not return to Stoatley Rough School in September. This rather abrupt response and swift and final closure of my time at this school left me feeling a double rejection. I had been rejected by the Nazis for being Jewish, and I had now been rejected by the Jewish community because one of its representatives had forgotten to check his diary, and those who had claimed to be responsible for my Jewish upbringing had decided to end their responsibilities because I had requested some thinking space. I made a major decision. The past was the past was the past. It would be put in a box and the lid tightly closed. Even as I write I realise that this may be a retrospective and adult way of verbalising it, but the decision was clear and, as far as I thought then, final.

CHAPTER 8

A New Beginning

Now in September 1946, as I discussed my future with Les and Vera, the religious questions that had got me into my present position temporarily faded into the background. There were more immediate problems to resolve, namely about my continuing education. The content of my education at Stoatley Rough, especially the lack of practical science, and the fact that my foreign-language subject had been German rather than French, made it impossible for me to return to the King Edward VI Grammar School where I had previously been. There was no level into which I could easily slot. Other options seemed equally problematic. Fortunately we found out that the local Worksop Technical College was about to open an entirely new course for anyone whose education had been interrupted for any reason during the war years. It would be flexible and tailored for individual needs, and it would lead to a Matriculation Certificate of the University of London. I immediately enrolled and found myself in a group that comprised others of my own age together with newly demobbed or invalided ex-servicemen. We were a motley crew. And we had an unusual timetable. Because this was a hastily put together course to meet an immediate need it had to fit in with the existing courses and timetables. So ours was a two-year, part-time course running intensively from 9.00am to 9.00pm three days a week, Tuesday, Wednesday and Thursday. It took a little while for my 15-year-old body and brain to adjust to this unusual style and intensity of study, for Mondays and Fridays were not just days off – they were given over to quite a lot of homework on those areas in which we were most lacking. In the summer of 1948 I matriculated in English, English Literature, French, Mathematics, Engineering Drawing, Geology and Physics, and so, in the coming term, I was able to return to the sixth form of my old school, King Edward VI Grammar, for the Higher School Certificate, which I achieved in 1950.

But all was not work. I greatly missed the sports and social side of Stoatley Rough School, so I took up long-distance cycling, whereby a few of us would cover a hundred miles a day in the Peak District of Derbyshire. I also took up rugby, and later hooked for Worksop Town during the 1949–50 season. In addition I became very involved in the youth group at St John's Church, Worksop, including their drama section. In the summer of 1948, on the lawns of Southwell Minster, we performed 'Tobias and the Angel', which was based on the book of Tobit in the Apocrypha, and in which I was cast as Raguel. Also at this time I joined the Air Training Corps (ATC), which gave me a real taste for flying. At one ATC camp at Church Fenton I was taken for a flight in a Tiger Moth and underwent the exhilarating experience of a whole sequence of aerobatics. Gliding was part of the ATC programme and I gained my A certificate as a glider pilot. Sadly, mainly due to time and financial constraints, this was a sport I was never able to resume.

Throughout this period my spiritual pilgrimage continued in a way that was probably deeper than for many my age and, after much thought, on 10 November 1947 I was baptised and confirmed in St John's Church, Worksop. On 2 September of that year the British Government granted me British citizenship, as it did for many others who came to this country with the Kindertransport.

I now felt that the various and many interruptions in my life were in the past, and in September 1950 I began a degree in Electrical Engineering at Nottingham University. I threw myself eagerly into many facets of university life. Very quickly the opportunity of hooking for the university Rugby XV presented itself, but this was dashed due to recurrence of an earlier back injury (sustained during a tackling demonstration while at Worksop Town) and I had to give up. I joined the Engineering Society and soon took on the responsibility of Committee Secretary. Involvement in both rugby and the Engineering Society led almost inevitably to a third recreational activity, so most Saturday evenings (and some other evenings) were spent in the Rose and Crown.

This lifestyle meant that I avoided all contact with organised Christianity on the campus, my excuse being that the Student

Christian Movement was far too liberal, the Anglican Society too high church and the Christian Union too holy. I did, however, attend St Mary's Church, Wollaton Park, on Sundays and became a Sunday school teacher there. The vicar and his wife kept an open house to all the students who worshipped there. Looking back we must often have outstayed our welcome and eaten more than they could afford.

Gradually I could feel my grip on my faith beginning to loosen, but events would prove that God was not going to let me go that easily. Every evening I maintained a time of prayer in my room, and every time I prayed God made it clear that I should join the Christian Union. I greatly resisted the thought but it just would not go away. It so happened that at this time we worked in pairs in the Engineering laboratories, and I was paired with John Busby, the then President of the Christian Union. We always worked together very well and formed a good relationship, but nothing of a spiritual nature ever entered into our conversation. But one day I could hold it back no longer.

'John,' I said, quite out of the blue, 'I think your CU is narrow-minded, bigoted, hypocritical and holier than thou. Please may I join?' His reply stunned me and still fills me with a sense of awe.

'Welcome,' he said, with no sense of hurt or anger at my accusations. 'Welcome, Henry. We've been praying for you.'

This clear demonstration of how God can work through the prayers of his people has never left me, though even now I do not pray as much as I should. My CU membership was reluctant, and at first I simply tagged it on to my other involvements without much change in lifestyle. Looking back I must have been its most embarrassing member, but I was always accepted and encouraged in my somewhat precarious faith.

Throughout this time my back injury was a continuous niggle and I became more and more dependent on painkillers. Eventually I was given a hospital appointment to see Mr Campbell, a consultant orthopaedic surgeon, who put me on a course of diathermy – deep-heat treatment. This was effective in the short term but was no real cure. I was then seen by a very new registrar who rather coldly said, 'Sorry, there's nothing more we can do – you'll just have to grin and bear it.' It was not just what he said but the way he said it that made me see red. I went through to the secretary's room, sat myself down in a chair and said firmly, 'I'm sitting here until you get Mr Campbell. If he says the same thing I will grin and bear it, but I'm not going to be spoken to like that by this arrogant young registrar!' I don't know what I expected her to do, but in next to no time I found I was being examined by the consultant, and within a very short time I was admitted to Harlow Wood Orthopaedic Hospital for spinal manipulation and five weeks of intense physiotherapy.

In the orthopaedic pool I succeeded in mastering what had constantly eluded me in the past despite much effort: I learnt to swim! I also took the opportunity to learn archery while I was there. The hospital was in Mansfield, at the centre of the Nottinghamshire coalfield. Most of the patients were therefore miners who had been injured in pit accidents and were, on the whole, much more seriously injured than I was. One exception was a fellow student who had contracted polio.

When I left hospital I felt I was walking on air; I had never been fitter in all my life. However I was advised not to play rugby again and so I resumed cycling. I remember one day cycling through a small area of Nottingham that was so deprived it took my breath away. I had been used to seeing slum areas in the Yorkshire and Lancashire towns, but I had never seen anything as bad as this. I did not know exactly where I was, and despite trying I never found those few streets again, but they left an indelible mark on my thinking. When, just eight years later, I spent some time in Northwood, a smart and prosperous area of North West London, I often remembered that occasion.

After a time I hankered to get back onto a sports field of some kind. One day I happened to see a game that was totally new to me – men's lacrosse. This was a fast-moving, exhilarating game with very few rules and therefore very few stoppages, but as it was a strictly no-contact sport it was just right for me. Also, because so few people played it there was very little competition to get into the team. The main drawback was finding other teams to play against, so it involved a great deal of travelling. The only other university to play at the time was Cambridge, and there were local leagues in the Rochdale area and Epping in North London. I find it sad that this game has not gained the popularity I think it deserves.

Never far below the surface was the subject of my faith and my lifestyle, which just would not go away. Eventually, after much inner turmoil, I said, 'OK, Lord, you win (again) – no more alcohol.' The change was surprisingly easy. Although in the past I had also been a smoker as well as a drinker, I had been so out of choice and for social reasons; I had never found either to be in any way addictive.

The next challenge came when Bruce Hunt, a very close friend in the CU, took me to a Passover *Seder*, a commemoration of Israel's deliverance from Egypt. The celebration included a very good meal, and the dramatic storytelling involved the drinking of four cups of wine, and on this occasion there was no non-alcoholic alternative! I shot up an arrow prayer and the answer was quick and clear: 'Henry, our controversy is not whether you drink or refrain from drinking: that's no big deal, as long as you don't drink too much! The real issue is whether you can stop fighting and learn a more ready obedience. Go ahead. Enjoy the wine, but just learn to live a bit closer to me, that's all I ask.' It was a wonderful evening and I have enjoyed many *Seders* since, but I didn't fully respond to the challenge and more divine battles were to come.

About this time my brother was completing his medical training and was about to register as a doctor. He had decided to anglicise his name from Gert Arthur Feige to Gerald Arthur Fieldsend, and it seemed sensible that I would do likewise. So, by Deed Poll, I changed my name from Hans Heinrich Feige to John Henry Fieldsend. Our forenames were direct equivalents but Feige to Fieldsend arose out of changing 'Fei' to 'Fie' and adding something reasonable to that.

During my time at university my foster parents moved from Worksop to Wakefield, so my cycling journey to and from home was greatly extended. However this move would have a great impact on my life, as Chapter 11 will reveal.

CHAPTER 9

National Service

I graduated in 1954 with a BSc. (Hons.) Elec. Eng. However, before I could decide the future direction of my career, there was still the two-year compulsory National Service to undertake, and I decided on the Royal Air Force as my first choice. I was accepted for officer training and that September, after 'kitting out' at RAF Cardington near Bedford, I joined 34 Yellow Squadron of officer cadets at RAF Jurby on the Isle of Man for three months. I enjoyed the course but on completion found myself among the 'borderline' cadets whose future would be decided by an interview (quite a grilling) by the station commander and a senior officer from the Air Ministry in London. This I failed and so, after being sent back to Cardington for regrading, I was posted to RAF Yatesbury in Wiltshire for training as a radar mechanic. This was a real comedown as Yatesbury had been condemned in the 1930s (although never totally closed) and, despite having been brought back into very active use both during and after World War II, it seemed that little had been done to it since! I was not looking forward to three months of winter there. As it turned out I need not have worried. I had been there for less than a day when a message came over the tannoy that I was to report to the guardroom immediately. With some trepidation and in complete bewilderment I reported as ordered and, to my utter amazement, was shown a signal from the Air Ministry that I was to return to RAF Cardington for immediate commissioning. Leaving Yatesbury was one of the easiest goodbyes I have ever said! It was too late to rejoin my previous squadron, who were by now well established in their training at the RAF Technical College at Henlow, near Bedford. I was therefore made Acting Electrical and Instrument Officer at RAF Upwood, in Cambridgeshire. This was no sinecure as Upwood was one of the most active bomber stations in service at the time. Two squadrons of Avro Lincolns (stretched Lancasters) were based there. One squadron always stayed home, while half of the second squadron was in Kenya attacking the Mau Mau and the other half was in Malaysia bombing the very active Communist infiltrators. As I had not yet been through the technical course at Henlow this was for me a steep learning curve, particularly as the home squadron was continually on preparation exercises for going overseas at short notice.

My early childhood in Dresden was by now almost forgotten, but I was not allowed to totally bury it. The Lincolns were equipped with the H2S radar bombsight that had been used so effectively over that city just ten years earlier. Overseeing the maintenance and tuning of these bombsights was part of my responsibility and one of our Lincolns won the RAF bombing competition that year.

One very dramatic incident remains with me from that time. One of the Lincolns was constantly giving a false reading on its gyrocompass. However often we swapped the compass for newly serviced ones the problem continued. One day, as the plane had just begun its take-off run, I said to my flight sergeant, 'I don't wish the crew any harm but I wish they would wreck that plane.' I had barely finished those words when the plane veered off the runway onto the grass. The undercarriage was retracted and the plane came to a shuddering stop on its belly. I felt physically sick until all the crew were safely brought out. It would be easy to dismiss this as 'just one of those things', but the cause of the accident was not so easy to dismiss. The resulting inquiry found that the highly experienced and long-serving flight engineer had uncharacteristically misinterpreted a rev. counter failure on one of the engines as complete engine failure. He then shut down all four engines and *ordered* the captain to abandon take-off. The captain, faced with 40 tonnes of pretty well uncontrollable aeroplane travelling at 100 miles per hour had no option but to take it off the runway onto the grass and retract the undercarriage. I do not believe in thought transference, but the whole episode still leaves questions in my mind.

I was hoping to have some overseas experience with the Upwood posting, but just before I was due to go I was transferred to the RAF Technical College at Henlow for my technical training.

The college trained technical officers for many of the world's air forces, so there were officers from most of the Arab countries as well as many from South America and the Far East. It was a fascinating time, and as I ended the course as top student I felt I had justified the Air Ministry's change of mind. From there I was posted as Electrical and Instrument Officer to RAF St Mawgan, a Coastal Command Station near Newquay in Cornwall. The main fleet comprised two squadrons of Lancasters, which at that point were used mainly for navigation training, but there was also a small associated unit called ASWDU – the Air–Sea Warfare Development Unit. After a while I was seconded as the officer in charge of first-line servicing of this unit, which comprised three Avro Shackleton marine reconnaissance aircraft (another development from the Lancaster bomber), two Sycamore helicopters and an old Avro Anson. It was a dream posting and I was able to do a lot of flying. The Shackletons were used mainly for submarine hunting, and sometimes we were able to exchange places with the submariners, going down in the submarines while the sailors went up in the Shackletons. With the helicopters we were developing the early winch rescue devices, and on completion these were incorporated in the newly reformed 22 Squadron RAF Search and Rescue unit also based at St Mawgan.

My life was also developing in other ways. I learned to sail with a small club at the RAF base, and with Newquay Sailing Club, sailing very sturdy clinker-built Redwings. I helped in the chapel at the base and formed a small Bible study group. I was also becoming increasingly involved in the big Sunday evening evangelistic outreaches in Newquay, which were sponsored by the local Elim Church. All this required increased mobility, so I acquired my first motorbike, an ex-US army 750cc Harley-Davidson, which I later upgraded to a 1932 MG-engined Morris sports car.

One particular incident played a great part in my spiritual growth. At Newquay Sailing Club it was traditional for everyone to exchange boats for the last race of the season. As the gun was fired to give us a five-minute warning, the owner of the boat our crew was sailing came over to say there were no lifejackets in the boat he had and so insisted that we give him the jackets we were wearing. Of course we should have retired, but stupidly we decided to race without them. As we reached the first buoy we were in third place, but then a sudden squall came. The first two boats capsized as they tried to jibe, so my skipper decided on a complicated loop to avoid the dangerous jibe. But just as he shouted, 'Ready about – lee ho!' a strong gust jibed us and I was catapulted into the Atlantic – with no lifejacket! I remember lying in the water quite calmly thinking, 'If this is the way I die, so be it! I'm ready!' Then I became aware that I wasn't just lying there; I was moving a little way behind the boat. It dawned on me that I had some rope in my hand. On being thrown out of the boat I must have instinctively grasped at a sheet. Thankfully I was able to work my way back to the boat, where I tapped my skipper on the shoulder and said, 'Please may I come back on-board?' My skipper was so surprised he nearly fell in with me. He had been so busy keeping the boat upright that he hadn't noticed I wasn't there! While all this was happening the safety boats had been so occupied with the other capsized craft that they hadn't noticed our plight. The sound of a gun firing from the harbour wall told us the race was cancelled. Of course we were stupid to have begun the race but the experience gave me some assurance that my life's purpose had not yet been completed.

CHAPTER 10

A Change of Direction

As my National Service drew to an end it was time to proceed with job applications. I was already wondering whether I was being called to ordination, and I discussed this with the chaplain at RAF St Mawgan, but he wisely suggested that I ought first to spend some time in the secular field of industry before following that up. I looked for openings in which my RAF experience would be beneficial and was accepted on to a research and development project with the Sperry Gyroscope company, part of the Sperry-Rand Corporation, which had a small branch in Brentford. At first I was not told the exact nature of the project. Following further security screening I was eventually informed that I was on a team developing the guidance system for an intercontinental ballistic missile named Blue Streak.

London life was to be a new experience. I found accommodation in Kew, which was near enough to my place of work and also gave easy access to Kew Gardens, offering a welcome escape from the vastness of London. Here I began to attend Kew Parish Church where, through a passing incident, I would learn a vital lesson for my future preaching. Every Sunday evening one man would drive his wife to church and collect her at the end of the service. One particular evening, having waited outside the church for an unusually long time, he crept into the back of the building and asked the verger, 'Hasn't the vicar finished his sermon yet?' To this the verger wryly responded, 'Yes, he's finished, but he hasn't stopped.' Maybe sometimes people wonder whether I really have learnt that lesson!

I saw digs as only a temporary measure and soon moved to a bedsit in Kings Road, Richmond. I was overjoyed now to have Richmond Park as well as Kew Gardens within easy reach. At this time I joined Holy Trinity Richmond, where there were many people of my own age, and where I soon found opportunities to help with particular ministries.

Work on Blue Streak proved interesting. However, we could not kid ourselves that we were involved in the wider work of 'space research'. We had a much more limited brief: to design a ballistic missile that could deliver a nuclear warhead with devastating destructive power and accuracy halfway around the world. Our small team was well aware of the potential consequences of the work we were doing, and during our meal breaks we had many long and serious discussions about the world and the meaning of life.

Following the end of World War II the Russians and the Americans had between them creamed off the best of the German physicists who had designed the devastating V1 and V2 rockets. Now, with the threat of the Cold War hanging heavily over it, the UK was having to play catch-up. In our team we were agreed that the work was important and had to be done, but subconsciously many of us wished that somebody else was doing it. Apart from our team leaders most of us had newly graduated from university, and our hopes and idealism for a better world were rapidly evaporating. During my time in Harlow Wood Orthopaedic Hospital, where I had experienced the benefit of newly developing electro-medical equipment, I had seen myself possibly working in this field. But now, given the tensions of the international situation, and limited resources, most governments prioritised research expenditure towards the armaments industry. There were of course some openings in the private sector, but these were few and far between and were snapped up by those who already had some research experience. In the electronics field there were big developments afoot. Although computers as we now know them were still 20 years away, and we were still working with thermionic valves, which greatly limited what we could achieve, we had started receiving some new things from the USA called transistors, which opened up a vast range of new possibilities. However, gaining a real understanding of the new circuitry would take many evenings of further study at night school. Consequently I found myself faced with conflicting demands on my time. I began to realise that my heart was no longer with my work but with my involvement in the life and ministry of the church. I was reminded of an interview I had had with a company that was designing a cockpit simulator for crew training for the newly developed Handley-Page Victor bomber. At the interview I was told that my interests were too many and too diverse; there was such pressure on the task that they wanted someone who would eat, drink and sleep on the job. Since then thinking about an efficient and creative work style has changed quite a lot.

The decision about the future direction of my work came to a head when we were told that plans were afoot to relocate our laboratory to Bracknell, a newly developing town that was rapidly becoming the 'Silicon Valley' of England. There were many good reasons for this move. For one thing, our present building was old and it had been difficult to achieve the sterile environment that our work required. We did have a basic form of filtered air ducted into our lab but it was not properly air-conditioned or temperature controlled, so sometimes we were working in temperatures in excess of 100°F. That was a good test for the equipment we were designing, but some days were so hot that the electronic instruments we were using ceased to function!

I had to accept that I did not have that clear and often dramatic calling to full-time Christian ministry that others I knew had received. But at the same time the seed had been lodged in my mind while still in the RAF; it was growing and would not go away. Was long-term 'niggling' any less real than the clear and certain calling of others? I talked about this with my vicar, Revd John Balley, and we agreed that others should judge the reality of my calling. Consequently he sponsored me to attend a three-day selection conference put on by CACTM, the Church's Advisory Council for Training for the Ministry, at Farnham Castle in Surrey.

At the conference there were about 25 to 30 candidates and five selectors: a bishop, three other clergy and one layman – a very genial and insightful farmer. On arrival, after settling into our rooms, we were divided into five groups for what was called 'a short informal discussion for about 15 minutes'. Our group was given the topic 'Is suicide ever a morally justifiable option?' We were young and, though we came from a wide variety of backgrounds, we already had firm ideas about many issues. Therefore it took us only about five minutes to agree a clear 'no' to the question. When we reported this to the selector who came to join our group he responded, 'So you would condemn Captain Oates of the Antarctic expedition?' There was no time to rethink our position, but we realised that this was just a kind of 'warning shot across our bows', and that simplistic, unconsidered responses would not get us through the selection process.

The whole conference was pretty intense, comprising discussion groups, the giving of short presentations and talks from various people, as well as individual interviews with each of the selectors. We lived together as one close-knit community for those three days, and by the end we felt the selectors must have got to know us pretty well. A short time later I received a letter saying that I had been recommended for training, so my next move would be to apply to theological colleges.

I decided to apply to two colleges. The first was the London College of Divinity (LCD), which was still in temporary accommodation in Lingfield, Surrey, having been bombed out of its London premises during the Blitz, but shortly to move into new premises in Northwood, Middlesex. The second was Oak Hill College in North London. My first interview was with Canon L.F.E. Wilkinson (Wilkie), Principal of Oak Hill. When I arrived we chatted informally over a cup of tea for what seemed to be a very long time, and I wondered when the 'interview proper' would begin. Then Wilkie said, 'Henry, may I pray for you?' Immediately I thought, 'Pray? Why no interview? I haven't got a place here.' How wrong I was. As he prayed I realised that I had revealed more about myself than I probably would have done in the context of a formal interview. Yet I did not feel that he had in any way trampled on my private space. Wilkie was just a natural people's man, a gifted pastor. I probably learnt more about pastoral relationships from that 'interview' than I did from all the pastoralia lectures in my college years. I was therefore surprised and saddened when he said to me, 'Actually the college is full for this coming year; have you applied anywhere else?'

'Yes,' I replied. 'The London College of Divinity.'

A TYPICAL SCENE IN LAB 14.

'If they have a place for you it would be best if you took it. If not, we'll find a place for you here, even if you have to sleep on the kitchen table!'

A couple of weeks later I accepted the offer of a place at LCD, commencing in September 1957. I then booked a meeting at work with our project manager to hand in my resignation.

'Oh,' he said. 'Why are you leaving? Where are you going next?'

'You may find it difficult to understand,' I replied. 'I'm leaving engineering behind and beginning to train for ministry in the Church.'

He looked at me with utter bewilderment. 'B***** h***!' he exclaimed. 'You're the third person our team has lost this way!'

WITH BEST WISHES FROM ALL YOUR
COLLEAGUES AT SPERRY'S

It transpired that though our team had not been all that long established, three of us, who had not overlapped and therefore not known one another, had become ministers in the Church. We, together with a fourth man from another part of the project, eventually met up during our years of ministry. I still have the farewell card my team gave me. In the sketch I'm dramatically blowing up one of our precious new transistors and prophetically wearing my future clerical collar.

CHAPTER 11

Back to College

I arrived at LCD, or St John's College, Northwood, as it was more frequently called, in September 1957. The first thing I remember after finding my room is seeing that the name label on the door read 'John Fieldsend'. My immediate reaction was 'Do I explain my name yet again?' Over the years, when I had entered a new situation, people had been told the 'new boy's' name was John. I found the repetitive act of telling them that I was known as Henry quite difficult. This was partly because in my teens I still had quite a strongly guttural Germanic 'r', which my English teacher at Stoatley Rough School so effectively corrected that my 'r' became something of a labial 'l'. So when I tried to tell people, 'My name is Henry,' what they heard was 'My name is Henley.' So when I saw 'John' on my college room door I immediately agreed with Zechariah, John the Baptist's father, that 'His name is John' (Luke 1:63).

I settled very easily back into college life, especially as one of my fellow students was Bruce Hunt, the friend who had taken me to the Passover meal when I was a student at Nottingham University (see Chapter 8). We both now looked forward to another four years of student life together, and though we had gone our separate ways for three years we picked up our friendship as though we had not been parted.

Despite the advice I was given at Harlow Wood Orthopaedic Hospital, I had played a few games of rugby in the RAF and I decided to see how I would fare in the College XV. After a number of games I found that this was a mistake, but to my great fortune one of the other students was a qualified and experienced physiotherapist. His treatment was swiftly improvised. He got four of the beefiest forwards in the team to have a tug of war, two on each side – and I was the rope!

On the whole life at LCD was fairly uneventful. At that time the evangelical movement within the Church was still very much on the defensive, and the training curriculum was not nearly as creative or imaginative as it is now. I had hoped, to be honest, that this would be a fairly short interlude in my life. The location of the college disturbed me: I had never lived in such an affluent area and once exclaimed, 'If I were not a Christian I might have

The LCD Rugby Team.

become a Communist!' Also, I just wanted to get on with the ministry that had so excited me at Holy Trinity Richmond. I had planned for the usual three-year diploma course, which was required for ordination, but with my degree background I could have got away with just two years. However I was persuaded by the new principal, Revd Hugh Jordan, to enter the Bachelor of Divinity (BD) course, which would take four years.

I became very friendly with a student named Colin Bedford, who was from Holy Trinity Church, Aldershot, a church with a very large and flourishing youth group called the King's Own Bible Class. They had over 100 teenagers who always went on a two-week camp during the summer holidays, and I was invited to become one of their leaders.

The first camp I joined was near Aberdovey on the Welsh coast, where we had two weeks of almost unbroken sunshine. The second was at Portscatho on the south coast of Cornwall, where we had almost ceaseless rain. Several events remain in my memory from that camp. The first two relate to the warmth and generosity of the local people. The best of tents and clothing do not withstand the combination of constant rain and young campers unaccustomed to the discipline that such camping requires. We almost had to curtail our holiday until the local bakery offered us the use of their ovens as they were cooling after the day's baking to dry our clothes. Maybe today's health and safety rules would not allow for such generosity, but it saved our camp and, as far as we know, the quality of the bread was not compromised! Also there was a cafe in the village run by two wonderful ladies who made the most delicious cakes. These were displayed around the cafe. The offer, written up clearly on the counter, was that if you bought a cream tea you could then eat for free as many of their cakes as you wished. This offer worked well for their general clientele but they had not bargained for about 90 hungry teenagers descending on the village. Unsurprisingly some of the more outspoken villagers told the ladies that they should not tolerate the way our campers took advantage of the offer, but to our surprise the ladies responded by loosely borrowing the words of Pontius Pilate: 'What we have written we have written,' and our campers remained free to patronise the cafe (although we persuaded them to moderate their appetites!).

It was at this camp that I was for the first time invited to speak at the evening epilogue. I cannot now remember the subject of my talk but I carefully prepared four points, outlined on four postcard-sized pieces of paper, each of which was carefully timed to last for five minutes. The talk went well and I retired to my tent well pleased. To my surprise next morning there was no loud wake-up call and the daily programme was running very late. On enquiring why, the response was, 'Didn't you realise? You spoke for nearly an hour!' My mind went back to the comment from the verger at Kew Parish Church (see Chapter

10). I record this because sermon length was an issue that was to crop at up at other times in various guises in the years to come.

Two things happened during my time at LCD that gave direction to my life, both in the short and longer term. The first thing, though I didn't realise it for a long time, was the start of a real acknowledgement of God's continuing covenant with the Jewish people. Initially I understood this in terms of 'with them'. It would take many years and many changes in my life before I understood this as 'with us'. The second was that I met Elizabeth, who was to become my love and my soulmate for the many challenges that, unknown to us, lay ahead. Just how we met is worth recounting.

Les and Vera, my foster parents, had settled at the parish church of St Helen's, Sandal Magna, in Wakefield. They were great Gilbert and Sullivan fans, and at one production in Leeds they found themselves sitting next to another couple from Sandal Magna – Cecil and Dorothea Coles. As parents do, they chatted about their offspring and it transpired that Cecil and Dorothea's elder daughter was a nurse at an RNIB Sunshine School, which happened to be in Northwood. Naturally I was told about this, and one day, while buying stamps at Northwood post office, my attention was attracted by a nurse with a group of visually impaired children. She was explaining to them about letters and stamps and postboxes and how the whole collection and delivery service operated. I felt that I had seen this nurse before in a different context, so I asked her, 'Are you Elizabeth Coles?' to which she responded in the affirmative. Not a very romantic beginning but the rest, as they say, is history.

As our relationship blossomed there were some very definite advantages and challenges for us. One advantage was that the Sunshine School terms pretty well coincided with our college terms, so we were able to spend term time and vacations together. By now I had exchanged my bicycle for a Royal Enfield 350cc Bullet motorbike on which we were able to travel up and down the fairly newly constructed M1 together. The Bullet was a bit of a comedown from the Harley-Davidson I had had in the RAF, but it served its purpose well. One of the challenges was that Elizabeth worked some difficult shifts, including a lot of night work, so, although her school was adjacent to our college, there were many periods when we did not see each other. In those days college discipline was pretty rigid and the hours during which female guests were allowed to visit were very limited. However the college principal, who with his wife was openly very encouraging of our relationship, made a room available in his home for us so we could spend some time together.

In the Sunshine School, Elizabeth, as senior nurse, was responsible for the development of the children's mobility and social skills (including basic skills such as eating) but she also had a concern for their spiritual development, for which no provision was being made. Many of the children went home for weekends, but quite a number did not. Elizabeth obtained permission from the head teacher, and from the parents, for some of our students to come in on Sunday afternoons to tell some simple Bible stories and teach the children some Christian choruses. We soon became known as the 'Sunday men'.

1961 was my final year at college and it was time to look for a parish in which I could serve my first curacy. The system then was pretty haphazard. The principal simply gave us a huge box of letters from vicars who were wanting curates, and we went through the box (hopefully prayerfully) and contacted the parishes we were attracted to, to arrange visits and interviews. Now some months earlier Dr William Greer, the then Bishop of Manchester, had visited LCD and made a big impression on me. I said to myself, 'I want to work in his diocese.' So when the first letter I looked at came from a parish in Shropshire I dismissed it as 'Shropshire! There are more cows than people!' This little incident was to come back to me later on, when Shropshire took a major place in my life. Hurriedly I searched through the remaining letters until I found one from a parish in the Manchester diocese. Suffice it to say that one lovely spring day found Elizabeth and me ringing the doorbell of Christ Church Pennington, Leigh, in the diocese of Manchester. Even before the vicar, Revd George Parkinson, opened the door I said to Elizabeth, 'We are coming here,' so clear was my conviction. We had a wonderful couple of days with George, his wife Molly and their lovely family, and with the churchwarden. We returned to Northwood in a very confident frame of mind, eagerly waiting for a letter of confirmation from the vicar.

One little incident at the time seemed to us to confirm that we were on the right tracks. On our way back to Northwood (which was hurried because Elizabeth was due to be on duty), just as we were driving over the top of a hill in the Cheshire countryside, the engine of our little Morris 8, which we had recently bought, cut dead. A quick inspection showed a failed petrol pump, so we coasted down the hill, hoping, to paraphrase Mr Micawber, that 'something would turn up'. At the bottom of the hill we just had enough momentum to coast into the forecourt of a little petrol station. I still remember very sheepishly asking the attendant whether he had a spare petrol pump for a 1939 Series E Morris 8. 'Yes, of course we have,' came the reply, as though I had asked for a packet of crisps, and in no time we were on our way.

My last term at college passed uneventfully, apart from final degree exams at King's College London. My four years of theological study made me a Bachelor of Divinity (awarded by the University of London) and earned me an Associate of the London College of Divinity (ALCD) diploma.

CHAPTER 12

Back into the Real World

Elizabeth and I were married in St Helen's Church in Sandal Magna, Wakefield, on 12 August 1961. Because we had no commitments until my ordination in late September, we were able to enjoy an extended honeymoon, limited only by our meagre bank balance.

Our honeymoon hotel in Scotland.

We had such confidence in our little Morris that we planned a very ambitious tour of the Scottish Highlands in a little 6ft 6in square ridge tent. The Highlands were beautiful though for most of the time the weather was, well, let's say - Scottish.

Elizabeth and I had agreed that whatever our circumstances, she would not pursue her own career so that she would have the time to provide a welcoming home for me and our future family, and anyone who had need of hospitality and support – especially any families in our parish who had children with special needs. This is her very special ministry and she has exercised it with love, warmth and great enthusiasm wherever we have lived.

I was made a deacon in Manchester Cathedral on 24 September 1961, and with the assurance of an annual stipend of £460, we were looking forward to moving into Priory House, the curate's house in Pennington. But a snag had arisen. The curate whom I was due to replace had not found another position to move to. He therefore remained in post for some time, meaning Priory House was not available for us. It seemed that we were homeless. At the eleventh hour, Leigh Town Council made one of their little two-up two-down council houses available to us. For us it was home though the house was challenging. An elderly widow had recently died there in a house fire, and the council had given it a quick coat of paint and a few rolls of wallpaper. But there were still several sheets of old linoleum on the living-room floor which, on removal, revealed damp and crumbling concrete. The council promised that the very next day they would send workmen to re-lay the floor. As it happened, our bed delivery had been delayed and we were sleeping on our sofa bed in the living room, so for the next few days we had to be up early and fold up our bed so that pneumatic drilling and concrete laying could take place around us. However we quickly settled in, albeit without knowing how long it would be before Priory House would become available to us.

This was our first experience of a typical Lancastrian industrial town, where most of the men worked down the coalmines and the women in the cotton mills. Life there was not easy but our neighbours, typical of that culture, were the salt of the earth.

Towards the end of November we had the joy of finding we were expecting our first child, though our happiness was shattered shortly afterwards when Dorothea, Elizabeth's mother, phoned to say that Vera, my foster mother, had died following a massive heart attack. Our distress was heightened when we heard that Dorothea had found Vera dead on the floor when she went round to visit. However this experience served in a very real way to draw our two families even closer together. Our son, Peter, was born the following July. By this time Les, my foster father, had retired from his post as Inspector of Mines and Quarries, and gone for a short period of training at St Deiniol's Library in Wales in order to be ordained to serve in the Wakefield diocese.

In the summer of 1963 my interest in the Church's Ministry to the Jews (as it was then named), or CMJ, was growing, and

Elizabeth and I, along with Peter, attended their annual conference at High Leigh Conference Centre. One of the speakers was Canon Peter Schneider, who was also a Jewish refugee from Czechoslovakia, and was now working in Jerusalem. Peter very strongly urged me to join in the work there, something I found very attractive, but on deeper consideration Elizabeth and I realised that after so many changes in my life I needed a longer period of stability before undertaking such a big move. I know Peter found my reluctance very disappointing, but I am more and more convinced that we made the right decision. We returned to our work in Pennington with renewed energy, but a long-term commitment to the work of CMJ had been established.

Almost invariably, one of the jobs a curate has to undertake is running the youth fellowship. Here the period of overlap with the other curate was a tremendous advantage because it gave me several months of benefiting from his experience in an area not well covered by my college training. Running a youth fellowship made up of very energetic teenagers in a primary school hall is inevitably fraught with difficulties. Footballs do get kicked hard and high and windows get broken. In order to maintain good a relationship with the head teacher I kept a stock of pre-cut pieces of glass and a tin of putty so repairs were completed before next day's school. Window replacement should be a part of every curate's training!

However one day the head sent for me with a complaint that nearly ended our use of the school. A series of deep indentations had recently appeared in one part of the school hall's new woodblock floor, for which I had no explanation. However the mystery was solved when I went into the school hall one lunchtime to collect something from our youth club cupboard. I first saw that the staff table was situated just where the indentations were, and then I noticed that many of the younger lady teachers were wearing the stiletto heels that had just come into fashion. The complaint was withdrawn and the youth club saved.

The eventual move to the curate's house came at an opportune time because our second child, Helen, was shortly to be born and the extra space was really a blessing. Altogether we spent three very happy and fulfilling years in Pennington, but all too quickly the time came for us to move on to my second curacy. Bishop Greer asked me to move to a very challenging position in the parish of Christ Church with St Luke's, West Didsbury in south Manchester. The very large parish with two churches was going through some problems. The elderly vicar was soon to retire and the bishop said that the experience of looking after the parish until a new vicar was appointed would stand me in good stead for the future. The move was not an easy one because, among other things, it meant moving into a very small terraced house where one room had to double up as my study during the day and Helen's bedroom by night. In fact other rooms had to become multipurpose too, and my electrical engineering background helped me to design and install an intercom and baby alarm system so we could keep an ear open to our children wherever they, and we, were! A further new experience for us was that we were living in a very multicultural area, with two synagogues and a redundant Methodist church that was to become a mosque. Most of the very large houses in what had formerly been a very prosperous area were now divided into small flats and bedsits. In every aspect of life and ministry we were on a steep learning curve.

Also in the parish there was a postgraduate club for overseas students where I was asked to be chaplain. At Christmas the club invited me to their celebrations, which were intended to let the students experience what an English Christmas was like. When I arrived I accepted a glass of cider and immediately a Muslim student challenged me, saying, 'Holy man drinking alcohol.' As I responded a group of students gathered round and we began a friendly but very animated discussion on issues relating to alcohol. The dinner gong was totally ignored until I decided we should, for the sake of the club, end the discussion. By the time we went into the dining room the food was not as the chefs would have wanted it to be!

After about 18 months the vicar, who was now almost completely blind, retired and, because of his disability, bought a house not far from the church. Normally this is something that is greatly discouraged but for us it proved very helpful. Very early one Sunday morning in April 1966, as I was preparing to go and take the early morning communion, Elizabeth went into labour with our third child. I was thankful that I could phone my newly retired vicar to stand in for me, because it was too late to find anyone else to take the service. The midwife turned up very quickly, and after a very short labour David was born. I was busily looking after Peter and Helen and was beginning to become slightly anxious, as nobody had thought of telling me that David had arrived. I was most relieved when the good news finally reached me.

As my two-year commitment to the parish was drawing to its close a totally unexpected invitation came from the parish of Christ Church Bayston Hill in Shropshire. Once again a possible move to Shropshire was not part of my agenda, so I went to discuss this with my bishop, confident that he would say, 'Oh no; we need all the clergy we can get in Manchester. We need you here and I've got something lined up for you.' However my misplaced ego was deservedly deflated as he actually said something like, 'Well, you might as well go.'

CHAPTER 13

A Reluctant Move

It was with somewhat mixed feelings and a lack of enthusiasm that in the spring of 1966 Elizabeth and I drove to Bayston Hill for a preliminary recce. What we found there did not raise our spirits. There was, at first sight, a small Victorian church with a few small cottages around a rather characterless common, and little else. We could not be certain where the vicarage was and, more importantly, where was the parish? Was this all? On leaving the common we crossed the A49 and found a relatively small, new housing development. We left the area, pulled into a lay-by and prayed.

A week or two later I returned by myself to meet with Revd David Shiress, the vicar of St Julian's church in Shrewsbury, who was responsible for the appointment, and with Revd Bob Griffin, who was still in post as the vicar of Bayston Hill. I began to see what was happening in the church and the potential there was. I also found which house on the common the vicarage was. It is best described by the question of a friend some years later who, having travelled by train through the village, asked, 'What was that castle-like building high up on a bank?' Eventually, after further meetings with the churchwardens, it became clear that this was the parish we should move to. We began to make the radical adjustments required by the move from a typical

Manchester terraced, back-to-back house to a six-bedroom house with two staircases and nearly three acres of garden. When we finally moved in October there was one aspect that we hadn't fully appreciated: there was no central heating. Therefore, the daily maintenance of four separate fires became part of our winter existence. The following summer we found that mowing the grass was pretty well a whole day's work.

One of the first things I noticed after we moved in was that the picture rails and other woodwork in some of the rooms were full of tiny holes. Woodworm! I was devastated. But on further inspection I realised that though the wood was peppered with holes the wood itself was still hard and solid – it didn't crumble away. No, it couldn't be woodworm, but what was it? On questioning, those who knew the long history of the vicarage and parish gave me the answer. During World War II the parish had had an alcoholic vicar who was also a leading member of the local Home Guard. (His alcoholism had begun with a breakdown following long service overseas with a leprosy mission.) When he was somewhat under the influence he saw not pink elephants but pink enemy aeroplanes, and he would sit in a chair and let fly with a double-barrelled shotgun! The plaster work had been repaired but the woodwork was still riddled with lead shot! The shot was doing no harm, however, so the wood didn't need to be replaced. Despite his limitations the vicar was a much-loved man with a heart of gold. During his time at

Bayston Hill the vicarage was always open to men in need, even if they had to sleep on planks supported on beer crates.

We quickly settled into the life and ministry of the church. The main Sunday morning congregation numbered about 50 people, including two senior staff from the nearby Shrewsbury School and their families, who were especially supportive. One of these families – Revd Michael Tupper, a housemaster and deputy chaplain of Shrewsbury School, his wife Jane and their children – was to have a great influence on the way things worked out, as we shall see later. And it was Jane Tupper who was to phone me about the appearance of my travel permit on *That's Life!*

The first 18 months were very much a learning and settling-in period, though even this was not without its surprises. On one occasion, for a particular piece of information I needed to read back numbers of our Parochial Church Council (PCC) minutes. To my surprise I found that a good number of the PCC had experienced even more reservations about my appointment than I had! In fact I had been appointed at the overruling of the bishop. There had been nothing personal about this. The parish had had two evangelical vicars and so there were those who wanted a vicar of a more central persuasion. To the credit of those who had felt this way, once I had, as it were, been imposed on them, they had accepted this with good grace, and I had no inkling that there had been this unhappy situation. However I realised that there was a work of healing that needed to be done.

Early the following year the Shrewsbury Council of Churches decided to prepare for an evangelistic mission, which they invited Canon Bryan Green to lead. I was very keen that we should be part of this, but it was soon made clear to me that between Shrewsbury and Bayston Hill there was a strip of green belt about a quarter of a mile wide, and neither the church nor the wider community of Bayston Hill would involve themselves in what was being planned 'in the other place'! However I was determined that such an isolationist policy should be overcome, and so we agreed to undertake a parallel mission at the same time, to be conducted by the very experienced evangelist Revd Dick Rees. On his preliminary visit, Dick quickly realised that what we really needed was not an evangelistic outreach to the village but a teaching mission within the church. However I did not want to be 'outdone' by what was to happen in Shrewsbury, so Dick, rather against his better judgement, agreed on the evangelistic direction.

About this time a new club called the Key Club began to meet informally on Friday evenings in one of the local pubs. By this time the village had grown to about 4,500 people. Housing was relatively cheap so we had mainly very mobile young, professional couples moving in. Many had moved away from their roots, and because they knew they would be on the move again soon did not put down roots where they were. Loneliness and boredom became something of a problem for some. The 'rules' of the Key Club were simple: couples would arrive at the pub, the men would put their bunches of keys into a bucket, and at the end of the evening they would be drawn out in a kind of lucky dip. Whatever bunch a man drew out, he would have that car, that wife and that house for the night. Those involved thought it would be a bit of harmless fun, but serious problems and break-ups inevitably developed. Much was swept under the carpet so there was little I could do, but it gave us a theme for the mission, which we would call 'The Key to Happiness'.

Despite good preparation and excellent work by Dick the results were deeply disappointing. As well as the main invitation meetings in the church, we had organised profession-based enquirers' home groups. One was for doctors, nurses and others involved in any kind of medical and social care. Another was for teachers and others involved in education. Yet another was for those involved in finance, commerce and so on. On the whole these groups and the main meetings were well attended, but what surprised Dick and ourselves was not indifference, which was fairly common, but an unusually high degree of open antagonism to the message and to the church.

The result of the mission was that there was practically no new growth to the church, and we lost a number of members who were perhaps half-hearted in their commitment. Our main congregation was reduced from about 50 to about 40 – not what we expected from an evangelistic mission! I realised that the gulf between our church and our wider community was far greater than I had thought. We were, in the eyes of many, an exclusive church that had little attraction for those outside. That needed to change, though at the time I was not at all clear how to bring this about. However, opportunities for change came very quickly – change that would affect our fellowship, my family and me personally in unimaginable ways, taking us in unexpected directions.

For Peter, Helen and David, living in such an enormous house had advantages as well as challenges. On the one hand there was plenty of space for each to develop their own interests and personalities. On the other hand, because of lack of space in the church, the children's groups had to meet in the vicarage so any toys left around were played with and easily broken. I quickly became an expert at toy repairs and Peter must have appreciated this because one day, as I emerged from my study at teatime, I noticed that he had brought all his friends' broken toys home from school for me to mend! He must have absorbed something of this because he is now a much better DIY man than I am.

Helen spent many happy hours playing in a large Wendy house that I had made, and, having absorbed much of Elizabeth's musical talent, would give a loud running commentary in song describing all that she was doing. This had disadvantages for her because even when we could not see her, if she got up to mischief we could hear her describing her misdemeanours in song. Helen now uses her musical gifts in teaching special needs children.

David happily whiled away the hours in the garden, developing both self-sufficiency and a love for nature. At a very tender age he would lovingly bring worms and other wildlife in from the garden and put them on the kitchen or dining room table. We all had to develop a taste for nettle soup and similar delicacies. The next step was to build a vivarium for keeping pet snakes and other reptiles, which had to be hidden away when some visitors came. David is now an environmental scientist.

CHAPTER 14

A Growing Church

Following the disappointment and bewilderment of the mission we spent some time seeking God's will as to a new direction for our church. How could we begin to make more positive connections with our wider community? Our prayers were answered in a way that left us reeling and working hard to keep up with all that he was beginning to do in our midst. Looking back there were three main areas in which we were being directed, and though they all seemed to be happening together I shall recount them in three separate chapters for clarity.

In the late 1960s and early 1970s the churches in our area were beginning to experience the charismatic renewal that had been greatly influencing many of the mainstream churches around the world for some years. Initially I had been very ambivalent about this movement, but now I felt that I should put my toes in the water. Whatever my reservations, one thing I knew: I and our church were desperately in need of new life. My first experiences reassured me that my reservations had been misplaced, and in 1973 three of us from our church attended the Second International Charismatic Conference, which was organised by the Fountain Trust and held at Nottingham University. The first conference had taken place in Guildford in

1971, but I had not been ready then. The fact that this one was taking place at my old university probably gave me the added confidence that we should attend. Immediately on arrival we knew we had come to the right place, and the conference was to have two major influences, one for our church, which I will expand on below, and also one for me personally, which I will discuss in Chapter 16.

Much of the worship at that conference, and a great deal of the teaching, was led by a group just over from Houston, Texas, USA, known as the Fisherfolk. In Houston they had developed an influential ministry based on the New Testament pattern of the Church as a close-knit family in which the love of God was shared in practical and supportive ways, and would overflow into the wider community. This was very challenging yet at the same time deeply attractive. I immediately felt a strong bond with the Fisherfolk and knew that they were offering the kind of teaching we greatly needed. Here was the answer to the failure of our previous evangelistic outreaches. We were strong on biblical orthodoxy but weak on living out the reality of life in the Spirit that the gospel offers. At the conference the Fisherfolk very generously drew me into their life, the outcome being that ours was the first church in the UK to receive their ministry. Here was the beginning of the transformation of our church. Inwardly we began to experience a deep love for one another, which could not but overflow beyond the walls of our church into the wider community. Eventually, after several moves, the Fisherfolk made their home with the Post Green Community at Lytchett Minster in Dorset. Through our fellowship with them many from our church began to go to the Post Green family camps every summer. These were tremendously encouraging for all age groups, but their youth work was especially memorable.

Quite naturally and spontaneously we experienced a time of rapid church growth, with many young families in our village coming to faith, and it was all happening without any conscious attempt at formal evangelism. The children's and the youth work grew very quickly and some gifted leaders moved into the village. This growth required both an increase and a broadening of gifts in our leadership team. In 1969 we had appointed Alison Woodhouse as a deaconess on our staff. Alison had spent some time with us on a placement during her training. We were pleased to have her back with us as she connected very well with our teenagers, and as a younger, newly qualified minister injected a good balance to our leadership team.

By now Michael Tupper was becoming more and more involved, and his gifted Bible exposition and teaching were greatly encouraging our growing congregation. One day, as Michael and I were out for a walk together, what seemed a chance remark brought a new and dynamic impetus to the development of our church. I said, 'Michael, I know it's not possible, but I wish you could become a full-time member of the team.' As soon as I said it I realised it was just an idle dream. How could Michael give up his important ministry? How could we justify and afford another full-time appointment? But to Michael, and to Jane, his wife, it came as a real challenge from the Lord. After much prayer and discussion Michael resigned from his post at Shrewsbury School, he and Jane sold their holiday cottage in Wales and bought a house in Bayston Hill, and Michael became our Associate Minister on an honorary, expenses only, basis. It was a huge change and a huge sacrifice for them, but they assure me they have never regretted it, and for the church it supercharged our development.

But, as is often the case, growth brings new challenges. Apart from the very old and somewhat dilapidated school building next to the church, which was used for the children's work, there was no place for the growing youth congregation to meet on Sundays. The vicarage was the only other venue for church activities and it virtually acted as our church hall. To meet the needs of a growing congregation we had the crèche in our dining room and Pathfinder groups in our kitchen and lounge and in my study. What was happening must have come to the attention of the diocesan authorities as one day my phone rang at one minute to nine. Intuitively I knew it was Stretton Reeve, Bishop of Lichfield. I don't know how he did it but when the bishop wanted to speak with me he always rang at one minute to nine.

'Fieldsend,' he said. (He was one of the more formal bishops who called his clergy by their surnames.) 'Fieldsend, I've heard from a trust that is administering a legacy for the building of a new church to be awarded by architect's competition. Appoint a good architect and get to work as speedily as possible. The diocese will pay his fees.' Now much of the new housing in our parish had been built on glebe land the diocese had sold to local builders, but a plot had been reserved for the eventual building of a church hall. Now the time seemed right to build a new church centre in the heart of the new housing area. Through his Shrewsbury School connections Michael Tupper knew an excellent architect who had been responsible for designing a revamp of the Shrewsbury House Youth Club in Everton, and we quickly gave him a brief. He designed a very beautiful and flexible church centre and constructed a detailed scale plan which I took to Church House, Westminster, for the competition judging on 17 July 1974. The reason I remember the date so clearly is because in the middle of the afternoon the streets of London were filled with the screaming sirens of police cars, fire engines and ambulances. It was the day that the IRA bombed the Tower of London. I returned to Euston station with some trepidation and sadness: trepidation because of the bombing and sadness because although we had come close, we had not won the legacy.

We had reached the point where not only was the church building totally inadequate for our growing congregation, but also the Pathfinders and other children's work had so taken over the vicarage that we even had a group meeting in the bathroom. Our church building could not cope with all that God was doing among us so we invited Revd Eddie Gibbs of the Church Growth movement to lead a weekend away so we could seek God's will for the future. By now we were at the top of the Diocesan Building Fund for New Churches and became very excited when our archdeacon asked to meet with our PCC. We met with great anticipation, but the archdeacon very quickly came to the point: the New Churches Fund had run dry. 'Never mind, Archdeacon,' said one of our members. 'We will go ahead without diocesan help.' I looked at the faces of our PCC and quickly realised he was speaking on behalf of all. The archdeacon left and we sat in stunned silence.

I realised that this was a kind of now-or-never moment when clear decisions had to be made. My first questions were, 'Are we agreed that God is calling us to this venture without any diocesan financial assistance? Do we realise the amount of money we shall need to find?' to which I got a firm, even enthusiastic, 'yes'. We adjourned the meeting so we could collect our thoughts and pray, and we reconvened in a few days' time. At this point I gave each member a piece of paper and asked, 'Will you, after a short silence and without any further discussion, write down the sum of money you think we should spend on this building. I know God owns the universe, but how far will your faith stretch? What should we budget for? We must do this without lessening our commitment to those ministries outside our church that we already support.' In silence I gave out 20 pieces of paper and collected them up a few minutes later. The result was mind-blowing. Each had the same figure – £150,000! This was one of those moments when one can only wonder and worship. Now £150,000 does not seem a large figure by today's standards, but back then it was a daunting challenge. Even so we realised that we could not be over-ambitious and would have to watch every penny if we were to have a building that would meet our expanding needs.

The first thing we did was to make our architect redundant. Then I started to contact a number of firms providing 'off-the-peg' church buildings. We visited several such churches around the country but were frankly unimpressed by what we saw. We also decided to contact a few local building firms to see whether any of them could come up with a complete 'design-and-build' package without the need for a professional architect. We did not honestly have high expectations from this direction but we felt that it was only fair to offer local firms an opportunity to be involved. As it turned out the answer to our needs came from a most unexpected direction.

A local building firm, whose two specialities were high-end holiday chalets and high-tech agricultural buildings, wanted to diversify and were keen to show us what they could offer. On the surface this link-up seemed totally ridiculous, but the firm had a brilliant design engineer, Len Taylor, who asked us for sketches showing what our needs were. He and his team spent hours meeting with us, listening to us and looking at our sketched plans. In the end Len said, 'I think I have an understanding of your requirements. I'll come back to you in a couple of weeks with plans of what I think you are needing – but I warn you, they will not be anything like what you have described to me.' When we met with him we were pretty sceptical about what he would come up with. He wasn't a member of any church. How could he understand our needs? But when he unrolled his plans we were overwhelmed. His design met all our needs, was wonderfully flexible and was very attractive in its simplicity. *And it was within our budget!* A friendly local architect, who had not wanted to accept the brief initially because he was too involved with other things, offered to become our honourary consultant to evaluate the plans and oversee the project. And so we were in business – except we had no money and absolutely no experience of fundraising on such a scale. We began with just one guiding principle, which was that our main thrust was to be direct giving from within our church membership.

In 1977 a house adjacent to our building plot came on the market so the diocese, glad to dispose of our large and rapidly deteriorating old vicarage, bought it, and with a minimum of alteration it became the new vicarage. The timely availability and proximity of this house seemed to affirm what we were doing.

The old vicarage was disposed of by auction, and Elizabeth and I, with our children, had the privilege of sitting beside the auctioneer during the proceedings. The house was bought by a Chinese businessman and his family, who immediately began to make major improvements that were to lead to another drama. One afternoon the peace of our quiet village was shattered by the sound of sirens and a multitude of emergency vehicles. Our doorbell rang long and loud and I opened the door to find a policeman and an Army sergeant with a 'Bomb Disposal Squad' insignia on his shoulders. I was immediately quizzed about the wartime history of the old vicarage. It emerged that the new owners were doing some major alterations on a rockery I had built at the end of the drive, and a JCB shovel had hit something that caused a loud explosion. The bomb squad had been called and they had discovered a cache of old cider bottles filled with a green, evil-smelling liquid of uncertain chemical composition, some of which had exploded on impact from the shovel. My visitors wanted to know whether I, as the most recent inhabitant of the property, could give some explanation! No, I couldn't, but further research showed that the wartime vicar had not only been free with use of his shotgun; he had made these 'anti-tank cocktails' and hidden them in a deep hole in case the German army passed that way. Fortunately for me, I had not dug deeply enough to disturb the munitions when I had built the rockery. As it was, I had put one prong of my garden fork through the bone of my left big toe in my enthusiastic digging, but at least I had escaped more serious injury.

When it came to planning the interior of the new church Len Taylor and I had many interesting discussions, with one another and with the diocese. Remembering that he came from an agricultural background, one particular conversation deserves highlighting. I was describing our plans for a baptistery, but the diocesan reps thought we were discussing a font. Len realised that we were not really communicating meaningfully. Suddenly his face lit up and he broke into the conversation. 'John, I get it. I know what you want. You want a sheep dip!' Henceforth our baptistery, once built, was called by that biblically relevant name. But unlike its agricultural counterpart it was beautifully tiled and plumbed into our central-heating system.

Throughout the planning and building process there was a tremendous sense of unity, love and anticipation throughout the church, and every decision of our PCC was unanimous. That is until we needed to order the chairs. I had borrowed specimen chairs from as many manufacturers as I could think of, and at

Rt. Rev. Keith Sutton, Bishop of Lichfield and Rev Michael Tupper baptising in the 'Sheep. Dip.'

one PCC meeting we moved on to the next chair every five minutes. At the end everybody preferred a different chair. The placing of an order was deferred until we were warned that we might be without any seating on the opening day. As we seemed unable to resolve the matter I had to cast what was literally the *chairman's* deciding vote!

At last, on 2 July 1983, the great day of our church's consecration arrived. Revd Eddie Gibbs, then National Training Director of Mission England, was to preach and the Rt Revd Leslie Lloyd Rees, Bishop of Shrewsbury, was to undertake the consecration. The sun was shining and everything looked good for a wonderful day. But then a series of tragedies began to unfold. At 7.00am the phone rang. At the other end, between sobs, Stuart, one of our church members, told me that Liz, his wife, had just died. Liz was a vivacious young woman who had tragically developed motor neurone disease, which rapidly took its toll. She had great artistic talent and had painted a beautiful frontal for our communion table. She had been in church, in her wheelchair, the previous evening, supervising its hanging. Now, on the day she had been so much looking forward to, she would not be with us, and for Stuart, and indeed all of us, this great day would be overshadowed by great sadness. I immediately went round to their house and there lay Liz, looking radiant, with all the contortions that had so afflicted her body totally gone. I prayed with Stuart but had to leave as there was still much to do before the afternoon's service.

As is often the case there were last-minute delays on the completion of the building. Most importantly the carpeting, which was to cover the whole floor area, had not been laid. The carpet fitters arrived at 9.00am, got down to work and at 10.30 went on their coffee break. By 11.00 they had not returned, and on enquiry I found that for some unknown reason they had gone on strike! Fortunately there were still some builders on-site who had sufficient experience and they completed the job, just in time.

The rest of the day went without a hitch and there was a real sense of wonder and praise for what God had enabled us to achieve. The figures on the final page of our dedication service bear witness. Building costs: £145,000. Giving from within the church membership: £94,000. Long-term loans from within the membership still to be repaid: £23,000. Income-tax rebate on covenants: £16,000. And we had built a versatile church building that seated 300 people, with specific areas for future extension built into the plan.

CHAPTER 15

A Caring Church

We had become a growing church but in order to fulfil the New Testament pattern we still needed to become a caring church. As so often happens when God wants us to learn a quality, he puts us in a situation where that quality is needed. So it was that in 1972 the Andrews family arrived from Cheshire. The reason for the move was that Susi, the youngest of their three young children, suffered from cri du chat syndrome, which very severely affects both physical and mental development. Her parents, John and Margaret, had heard that there was a renowned orthopaedic surgeon at our nearby orthopaedic hospital who, if it were at all possible, would help Susi to walk. To facilitate the move John had successfully applied for the post of Assistant Headmaster at the local Priory Boys Grammar School, and the family had arrived in Bayston Hill with great hopes.

However when Elizabeth and I first met John and Margaret their world had just fallen apart, because at their first hospital consultation they had been firmly told by this same surgeon that nothing could be done for Susi; she would never walk, and in any case, her severe mental limitations would render any surgical intervention meaningless. As Elizabeth and I listened to their story, and later shared it with other leaders in the church, we felt clearly that this was a prayer challenge, so every

Wednesday afternoon Elizabeth gathered a small group to pray with Susi and her mother. The great day came when Susi, hand in hand with her parents, *walked* into the orthopaedic surgeon's consulting room. In amazement he took Susi on for a series of operations to realign her ankles and improve matters even more. The prayer continued and so did other developments. As a family we had Susi to stay with us for short periods to give John and Margaret and their other children some respite. We still had to accept that Susi had severe difficulties, both physical and mental, and we began to be concerned for her long-term future. Elizabeth, with her background working with people with special needs, investigated the possibilities. She soon found out that there were facilities for people with severe physical disabilities and there were facilities for people with severe learning disabilities, but there seemed to be nowhere for people with both. The organisation that best fitted Susi's needs was L'Arche, but while they had suitable provision in France and other countries, they did not have any in the UK and were not planning any in the near future. As far as we could find out, in the UK those with multiple disabilities were ending up in rather stark institutional care. We all felt that this could not be right, for Susi was a lovely girl with great character and a loving heart. We began to realise that there must be other families with the same problem, so if a suitable long-term home for such people did not exist then, at some stage, we would have to build one!

But how should we go about this? Where should we begin? We researched other churches that were running caring projects of any kind to see what we could learn, and we also looked into whether the housing association model could give us any direction, but nothing met our need.

At some point I attended a regional conference in the West Midlands on the theme of cooperation between professional services and the voluntary sector in the care of the disabled. There I discussed Susi's situation with the director of Shropshire Social Services, but found no encouragement that her particular needs could be met. Time was passing; Susi was growing up and we felt that we would just have to launch out on our own. We told Shropshire Social Services of our intention and they obviously realised that we were serious, calling a case conference. Dr Michael York-Moore, a consultant psychiatrist at Lea Castle Hospital in Kidderminster, whose responsibilities occasionally took him into the Shrewsbury area, was among those present. I had met him briefly at the regional conference and felt some affinity with him. In his opening comments the director of Shropshire Social Services said he always welcomed the help that churches and other voluntary agencies gave, but in his opinion these agencies did not have the expertise to build and run a home, and they should leave this to the professionals. It was at this point that a most dramatic thing happened. Dr York-Moore caught the director's eye. 'Mr Chairman,' he began, 'in general principle I agree with you, but there is one exception, and that exception is Christ Church Bayston Hill.' I have no idea what made him say this. I have no idea how much he knew about our church. He lived many miles away and rarely came into the area, and I had had only brief contact with him. However to us it was a word of great encouragement. We were now even more assured that this was the right course of action.

Shortly after this the Andrews family went on holiday to the Bournemouth area. They returned in a state of great excitement. While there they had attended a church that really cared for the disabled, and the church had links with an organisation called Christian Concern for the Mentally Handicapped (CCMH). There was a leaflet explaining the work of CCMH, which described a couple of homes they ran in the UK. I quickly contacted their director, Revd David Potter, explaining our position, and early in 1983 he came to Bayston Hill to visit us. David explained that at present CCMH had no experience in working with people with severe or multiple disabilities, but he was very open to working with us to venture into this new field. He explained the way that CCMH worked. The initiative for any new home had to come from a local church, which would be responsible for raising all the building costs and showing that there would be continued interest in and support for the day-to-day running of the home. However, in order to guarantee security and continuity, the ownership of the properties would be vested in CCMH, which would be ultimately responsible, in cooperation with the sponsoring church, for all matters regarding the running of the home. Their homes were planned as small units providing a homely Christian environment, and were intended to give residents security for life, unless of course more specialised hospital care was needed. We visited a home run by the charity in Aberystwyth, and it became clear that this was the way forward for us. Over the following months we worked out some of the detail, and by July 1983 we had agreed the plans and were ready to put them to tender. Then the real work began. Following our intense fundraising programme for the new church building, we were now involved in finding an even bigger sum – £200,000! However, as this was a very different kind of project, our strategy was very different in that we would make applications to some of the big grant-aiding trusts and would welcome fundraising by all supporting friends. There were several hair-raising times when there were insufficient funds to make the stage payments. We asked the builders to slow down, but they seemed to have more faith than we did and continued at their fast pace, believing that we would be able to do a financial catch-up in due course, which in fact we always could.

It was with great joy and a sense of real achievement that the home was completed in 1988. But what should we call it? One name clearly presented itself. During all the years of preparation and building Dr York-Moore would drop in with a word of encouragement whenever he was in the area. Sadly he had died in April 1987 shortly after his retirement, so as a tribute to his unstinting support we decided to call the home York House, and we were delighted that his widow was able to come and plant an oak tree in his memory. We had fulfilled our commitment to Susi and were able to offer a lifetime commitment to eleven other people with severe multiple disabilities who would otherwise not have found this kind of home available.

York House under construction alongside the new Christchurch

During these years there were plenty of other opportunities to show caring love in the community. Wherever possible, Elizabeth would organise support in many and varied ways for parishioners in real need. Others turned to us with a great variety of problems requiring personal counselling, so Jane Tupper, who had a natural gift in this area, and I went on several training courses with the Clinical Theology Association in order to provide a more skilled service in this direction. This naturally led to new and unexpected developments in my life, which will be the subject of the next chapter.

CHAPTER 16

Personal Changes

I now return to the other and more personal influence that arose out of the Second International Charismatic Conference in Nottingham that I mentioned earlier. While we were in Manchester Elizabeth and I had done some training in pastoral counselling, with an emphasis on healing of memories, with the Clinical Theology Association, directed by Dr Frank Lake. Now, in our growing church, there was an increasing need for this kind of ministry as more and more people with deeply troubled pasts were joining us. At this time Elizabeth was very occupied with our three young children and with looking after a very large vicarage, which was also the hub of nearly all that was happening in the church. Consequently Jane Tupper and I were mainly involved in this ministry. Dr Lake had been one of the speakers at the Nottingham conference, and this led Jane and I to begin to attend his training courses.

Then it all happened! The crunch point came when I woke up one morning with this question in my head: 'Hey, I'm Jewish! How on earth have I got here?' It had come from nowhere, and I quickly realised that this was not just an academic matter. The question had pierced right into the heart of my being and pulled me into a deep identity crisis, which took the form of a long, dark tunnel. I was dominated by wondering, 'Who am I?' and could find no answer. On a practical level my inward confusion meant that I could hardly function outwardly. Elizabeth and my family were very supportive, as was the church, though they must have found my situation difficult to understand. A small but dedicated group met regularly with me to pray for me.

I had previously booked into a Clinical Theology Association training conference at Nottingham University and still felt able to attend. However within an hour of arriving the dynamics had changed: I was no longer there as one of Dr Lake's students but as one of his clients! Having explained my background to him I said, with real pain but also genuine commitment, 'Frank, whatever it takes and however much it hurts, I want to know who I am. I don't want any area of my life blanked off, nor any dark cupboard I dare not open.' Gradually light appeared at the end of the tunnel, and after several tearful counselling sessions I re-entered the light, still very much a follower of Jesus but now also a *Jewish* follower of the one who is my true Messiah. No longer was I a Christian who had a Jewish background; I was a Jewish Christian, a Messianic Jew (though I did not actually come across that title for another year or two).

I have to admit that I did have reservations about some aspects of the Clinical Theology movement, and I found elements of my relationship with some of their staff members quite difficult, though that probably says more about me than about them. However Dr Frank Lake was God's gift to me and I shall be eternally grateful for his deeply insightful and precious ministry. The climax of this came at the close of one conference, when there were still some people with unfinished business who needed further ministry. Frank said to us all that he would continue until everything was concluded, but that he did not like to work alone and would be grateful if someone could spare some time to remain with him during the ministry. I did have time and just made myself a quiet support while Frank ministered. We were there for probably another three or four hours, and I can say with confidence that I learnt more in that time than from all the lectures and seminars before or after that event.

The outworking of this whole experience challenged my life on three fronts. First it challenged my identity with respect to my membership of two groups whose relationship was at best strained and at times antagonistic: the Jewish and Gentile communities at the secular level, and Church and Synagogue at the faith level. Secondly it challenged my identity in terms of my nationality. I had not only become a *Gentile* Christian; I had become a *very English* Christian. Now I needed to reinherit not only my Jewish identity but also my Czech-German identity. Now I had to re-evaluate and rebalance my understanding of both European and Middle-Eastern politics. But there were also some clear positives. My experience greatly enriched my ministry and the church wonderfully appreciated and encouraged my increasing insights into the Hebrew Scriptures – no longer was it just the 'Old Testament'.

In connection with all that was going on in my life I have to backtrack to another part that I have not so far mentioned. I have to go back to my time at Nottingham University, to the Passover *Seder* I mentioned in Chapter 8. Although at the time it did not arouse any strong Jewish identity issues for me, it was my first contact with the Hebrew Christian Alliance of Great Britain (HCA), which was to greatly influence my life at a later time. I cannot now remember the exact circumstances by which I regained contact with the HCA, but it must have been in 1967 that Elizabeth and I decided to go to their summer garden party in North London. I remember the occasion very clearly because as we arrived in our old VW camper van we were almost lynched by an irate group who accosted us with the question, 'What kind of people are you to come here driving a Volkswagen?' Though a refugee myself it was the first time I had met a refugee group whose memories and emotions were still so raw that simply seeing a fellow refugee driving a Volkswagen could cause such a strong reaction. Perhaps this marked the beginning of me 'owning' my Jewishness – when it began to re-enter into the heart of who I really was. Despite the VW incident I soon found new joy in being with my own kith and kin, spiritually speaking, and the strong reaction that the camper van generated was never repeated.

Perhaps I need to say for some readers that the Hebrew Christian Alliance of Great Britain (now called the British Messianic Jewish Association, or BMJA) began in 1866, and founded the International Hebrew Christian Alliance in 1925. The purpose of the HCA was to create a space where Jewish men and women who had begun to believe that Jesus was the One foretold in their scriptures to be the Messiah and Saviour could enjoy fellowship together. In belief and in practice we had become Christians and full members of the Church, but at the same time we still desired to observe the biblical festivals and other aspects of our Jewish culture without any compromise to our newfound faith. There was never any intention of the HCA becoming a church or a denomination. Indeed as the HCA developed its members became a valued part, and sometimes leaders, of their local churches. In time I became a committee member of the British HCA and was Vice President for a period of some years. In the 1960s and 70s some major stirrings arose, beginning in the American Alliance but spreading to the UK and elsewhere in the succeeding years. Through the interplay of many events a growing number of young Jewish men and women, without direct church influence, came to faith in *Yeshua* (*Yeshua* being the Hebrew form of Jesus). Of these, many also had little Synagogue background and were in the situation of having a new living faith without anywhere to naturally root into. Many felt little or no affinity for the mainstream churches, and yet found they needed something like a fully functioning congregation. The term 'Hebrew' had for some time been seen as rather archaic, and as early as 1915 the HCA of America had changed its name to the Messianic Jewish Alliance of America. About this time the return of Jerusalem into Jewish hands in 1967 created a new sense of destiny throughout the Jewish world, including Messianic Judaism. Consequently Messianic congregations began to be established and the Union of Messianic Jewish Congregations (UMJC) was born, with an initial membership of 19 congregations. In a statement in 2005 the organisation's delegates defined the UMJC thus:

The Union of Messianic Jewish Congregations envisions Messianic Judaism as a movement of Jewish congregations and groups committed to Yeshua *the Messiah that embrace the covenantal responsibility of Jewish life and identity rooted in Torah, expressed in tradition, and renewed and applied in the context of the New Covenant. Messianic Jewish groups may also include those from non-Jewish backgrounds who have a confirmed call to participate fully in the life and destiny of the Jewish people. We are committed to embodying this definition in our constituent congregations and in our shared institutions.*

The energy of these developments soon crossed the Atlantic and the growing London Messianic Fellowship decided to transform into the London Messianic Congregation (LMC). As far as the UK scene was concerned, this was entering into uncharted waters, so it was decided to invite a Messianic pastor over from America. For various cultural and other reasons, this did not work out and the LMC splintered and closed. Some of the members asked me to head up a new group, which we named the *Beit Shalom* Messianic Congregation. (*Beit Shalom* means 'House of Peace'.) We began meetings on *Shabbat* (Sabbath) mornings at Simeon House, the CMJ premises in North London. We were a small and rather disparate group, more united in what we did not want (i.e. what the LMC had turned into) than in what we were called to become. We enjoyed several years of good fellowship and some growth together, but for me it became increasingly clear that with my other commitments I could not give enough time to lead and keep united a congregation whose membership wanted to move in different directions. At the formation of *Beit Shalom* I had made it clear that my other responsibilities would have to take priority, and after one particularly difficult situation it became clear that I should relinquish leadership. Shortly after this the congregation disbanded.

My involvement with the BMJA continues, and I had the privilege of being part of the small delegation that attended a meeting of the International Alliance representatives in Puerto Vallarta, Mexico, in 1997.

CHAPTER 17

Family Reunion

Towards the end of 1984 one of my brother's patients in Sheffield flew to Atlantic City, New Jersey, USA, on a business trip. In the taxi on the way to his hotel the driver said, 'Hi, you're from the UK; I can tell by your accent. Whereabouts are you from?'

'From Sheffield,' the man replied.

'Sheffield,' the taxi driver repeated. 'Do you know of a Dr Fieldsend?'

'Why, yes,' he affirmed. 'He's my doctor. Why do you ask?'

'Well, I'm his cousin,' the driver revealed. 'I'm the daughter of his father's sister.'

When my brother told me about this I was blown away! How many taxis are there in Atlantic City? If this is *just* a coincidence what are the odds? Although we had had some contact with Edith in the post-war years, over time we had drifted apart and lost touch with one another.

My first thought was that we must visit as soon as possible. To my great disappointment Arthur wasn't greatly interested and did not want to go. We all have our different coping mechanisms when faced with past pains. My brother and I had coped for all these years by burying our memories. For me, recent experiences meant this was no longer a viable option. For Arthur the news only served to deepen his denial. Elizabeth and I decided we greatly wanted to go regardless, so I shared my news with my bishop, who gave me six weeks' special leave (unpaid!).

I wrote to Cousin Edith, the taxi driver in Atlantic City, and to Uncle Alfred, my father's brother, who lived in Los Angeles, California, and we arranged a programme. We were to stay for three weeks with Uncle Alfred in Los Angeles. Then we would fly to Atlantic City to spend a week with Cousin Edith before spending a week in Cherry Hill, Philadelphia, with her brother, Harry (formerly Horst), and his partner, Sharon. After that we planned to spend a week with friends in Washington DC before flying home.

So on 15 April 1985 Elizabeth and I flew out to California. For Elizabeth it was her first long-distance flight and though for me the experiences was not new, flying in a Pan Am Boeing 747 was very different from the Lancasters, Lincolns and Shackletons I had been accustomed to. It was a beautiful day and we had wonderful views of Scotland, the ice caps of Greenland, the Canadian tundra and the Canadian and American West Coast Rockies. The only hitch was that the Los Angeles customs officers were on strike so we had to land, disembark and go through customs in San Francisco, then reboard for the short hop to LA.

On exiting from passport control and baggage reclaim there was a shout of 'John!' and there was Cousin Larry, Alfred's son, whose existence we had not even known of a few months ago. Soon we were engulfed with hugs and kisses, and Alfred, whom I had not seen for almost 50 years, remarked to me, 'Don't you look like your mother?' Helen, Alfred's wife, who regrettably was confined to a wheelchair, and Melody, Larry's wife, completed the reception party. Soon we were speeding in Larry's huge station wagon through unfamiliar land and cityscape to the Farmer's Daughter Motel in Fairfax, which was to be our home for the next three weeks. We felt very privileged that the family had gone to such lengths to give us such a generous welcome, and we knew then that we would have a good time together.

Very quickly we became aware of muted and muffled conversations on the phone. We soon realised that our cousins in Atlantic City and New Jersey were phoning with urgent questions as to what we were like. It became clear to us, though it was never stated, that their mental image of a Christian priest was based on a rather narrow and dated picture of a typical Spanish-style Roman Catholic priest. Much to their relief we arrived very informally dressed with me in an open-necked shirt; I had not even taken a dog collar with me.

The motel proved very comfortable, with its own swimming pool, and every morning we wandered through the huge neighbouring farmers' market, which sold many delights to tempt us for our breakfast. On most days Alfred would collect us and drive us around the endless sights of Los Angeles. We visited Hollywood, Santa Monica, Sunset Boulevard and many other well-known places. We realised that Los Angeles was not just one city but a complex of several cities that worked and lived as one. We also did quite a lot of exploring by ourselves, one day taking a Greyhound bus to Sea World in New Mexico. Our family and their friends were astounded that we actually *enjoyed* walking; it was difficult to persuade them that we didn't want to be driven everywhere.

Before our visit we had already contacted Richard and Beverley Paine, who were old friends from the Fisherfolk community. They were otherwise engaged on our first Sunday in LA, but Beverley's sister Diane took us to All Saints Episcopal Church in Beverley Hills, a very fashionable church yet wonderfully welcoming with a real sense of commitment.

One time Alfred drove us to visit some friends of his, also originally from Germany and now living in the beautiful town of Santa Barbara. It was interesting to have another perspective from someone who had realised the gravity of what was happening in Nazi Germany and had decided to leave while that option was still easy. As well as many memories shared, an interesting part about that visit was that, though nothing was said, the reading matter supplied for visitors in their loo was a pile of *Jews for Jesus* magazines.

Another day Alfred's daughter-in-law took us to experience Los Angeles' Mexican quarter. After mango on sticks for elevenses we were taken to her favourite Mexican restaurant for lunch and excitedly introduced to the owner as her cousins from England. With a typical Spanish welcome we were guided to a table and had to sample a little of almost everything on the menu. Afternoon tea was taken in one of Los Angeles' top stores and then, just as we were ready to settle down to a quiet evening, we were taken out to dinner in a superb fish restaurant! Such is American hospitality!

By now we were beginning to feel a bit more adventurous so we hired a car for the day. We drove east, right across LA to San Bernardino, and then we climbed up into the San Gabriel Mountains to Lake Arrowhead and Big Bear Lake. Our surroundings made us feel we were part of a real Wild West movie! The following Sunday was a glorious summer's day and we decided to walk to church, a three-mile stroll through some of LA's most beautiful scenery. After the service Alfred met us and took us home for brunch, and then we drove through more breathtaking scenery up to Mount Wilson Observatory with its famous 100 inch telescope. From there we saw hang-gliding on an American scale – from 5000 feet up on the mountain, landing 10 miles away in Victoria Park, Pasadena!

Amid all this the real reason for our visit was not overlooked. Alfred and I had some deep and heart-searching conversations as we began to unravel how it was that we had lost contact after some brief letter exchanges after the war. In 1937 Alfred, who was not then married, had managed to get to Montevideo in South America on a bogus business trip. From there he had worked his way up to Los Angeles where he had obtained a temporary residence permit and eventually US citizenship. From there he had managed to get Edith, his niece, a permit to come to the US as a minor (she would have been about 15 years old at the time). Alfred repeatedly and emphatically reassured me that he had done his utmost to get our family out of Europe to the States, but following the infamous Evian Conference of July 1938, US immigration would not budge on its very limited quota and he could not get us in. For all these years Alfred had thought that Arthur and I had ended the relationship because we held him guilty for not trying harder to get our family to the USA. Arthur and I had a very different perspective. We were convinced that Alfred had cut us out because we had been baptised as Christians. In fact the real reason was much more prosaic and to that extent much more tragic. The real reason was that we were all too busy getting on with our lives and correspondence was not very high on any of our agendas. Once that was cleared up we had a very easy and warm relationship. As I have involved myself more and more in the field of survivor stories I have found this to be an almost universal factor: we men are not very good at letter writing and maintaining relationships, and where relationships have been maintained there are usually women doing the spadework. It's a lesson I have learnt in my head but I have to admit that I'm still not very good in practice.

There was one other relationship that Elizabeth and I were able to renew during our time in LA, and that had nothing to do with my family. Eddie Gibbs, who had had so much to do with the growth of our church in Bayston Hill and who had preached at the dedication of the new building, was now heading up the church growth department at Fuller Theological Seminary in LA. We were able to spend a little time with him and his family, and he took us to the Presbyterian church where they worshipped. The normal Sunday congregation was about 6000 and membership came from quite a wide area so there was a very large car park. But the church was not resting on its laurels; it had taken Eddie on as its church growth consultant and the plan was to take the whole vast car park underground so that they could build a larger church above it! Here I have to admit to some racial bigotry on my part. In England I have often found American visitors a bit too large and too loud. But in their own vast country they are much more to scale, and I found their huge enthusiasm for life and their endless vision of what could be accomplished with commitment and hard work a real challenge to my more quiet and restrained attitude to life.

There were of course things that were not easy to get used to, especially the number of guns being carried by people other than the police. Our motel manager had a gun on his belt much of the time. The manager of the local 24-hour supermarket carried a gun on his belt after 11pm.

Our time in Los Angeles had to come to an end and on 2 May we flew to Atlantic City. The flight was memorable in that there was severe weather as we approached New York, and we flew a diversion over Lakes Michigan and Erie. We then had a very bumpy flight to Atlantic City in a small De Havilland Dash 7! Cousin Edith, the taxi driver, and her husband, Ernest, met us and took us to the motel that was to be our home for the week. We were later introduced to their three children and two grandchildren.

Almost everybody in Atlantic City seemed to be involved directly or indirectly in the casino business, and though we were there to try to rebuild family we found we had very little in common. One day we took a coach to New York and decided that the best way of seeing the Big Apple in one day was to take a coach tour round the city. The scale of everything was overwhelming; from arriving at a multistorey coach station to the view we got from the top of the Rockefeller Center. Perhaps the most memorable sight was the large *menorah* beside the high altar in the Cathedral of St John the Divine, the largest cathedral in the Western world, which is not due be completed for another 100 years. The *menorah* was a gift from New York's Orthodox Jewish community. We were fortunate to visit on Vietnam Veterans' Day and passed through masses of computer tape floating down from skyscraper windows. We were told on the coach commentary that these ticker-tape parades would soon be a thing of the past as skyscraper windows were being sealed to prevent people jumping from them!

From Atlantic City we went to Cherry Hill in Philadelphia to spend a week with Cousin Harry and his wife, Sharon. This was a hectic but wonderful week, as the four of us got on so well together – as though we had known one another for years. Harry had trained as a teacher after coming to the USA, and since his retirement he had been an official guide in Philadelphia. We really saw the sights, including the Liberty Bell, as well as having a wonderful meal in Chesapeake Bay and seeing a great deal of New England. However Harry, who had survived internment in Bergen-Belsen concentration camp, didn't talk much about his experiences. Harry and Sharon subsequently visited us in England several times, but then sadly in 1999 Harry died from cancer.

After five weeks of intense but wonderful family times we travelled by train to Washington DC to spend the last week of our time in the United States with friends we had known in

Birmingham who were now working with CMJ USA and lived in Fairfax, Virginia. We spent a good couple of days touring the city, including of course the White House and the Smithsonian Institution, and then, on the Saturday, they took us to Beth Yeshua Messianic Congregation in Montgomery Village, Maryland. This really showed us how well Messianic Judaism was established in the States, and how naturally *Yeshua* fitted into his Jewish setting not only in New Testament times, but also in the 20th century.

CHAPTER 18

Family Celebrations

After our return from the USA it took a little while to readjust to life in a relatively small English community. In all our years of marriage Elizabeth and I had never been abroad before our six weeks stateside, but now, to our great surprise, we had developed a little wanderlust. It did not take long to start planning our next adventure! The next year, 1986, was to be very special in that we would be celebrating both our silver wedding and Elizabeth's parents' golden wedding. In view of all that was happening in our lives, where better to celebrate than in Jerusalem? However we did not want to book with an organised tour; we very much wanted it to be a special family celebration. From her earliest years Elizabeth's parents had taught her to respect the Jewish people and that they had a special place in the plans and purposes of God. Now this early teaching was bearing fruit in her life.

But how realistic was it for me, who had never visited Israel, to plan such a tour? I was closely involved in the work of CMJ, who organised excellent tours of the land. Would it not have been much simpler just to join one of these? Having opted out of this route we still decided that CMJ's guest houses in several centres in Israel would form the basis of our visit. We focussed our accommodation on CMJ's Christ Church Guest House just inside the Jaffa Gate in Jerusalem; the Church of Scotland's guest house in Tiberias, Galilee; CMJ's Stella Carmel Guest House on the top of Mt Carmel; and CMJ's Beit Emmanuel Guest House in Tel Aviv.

We began with several days in Jerusalem, then booked a hire car for the next stage of the journey up to Galilee. As I was leaving the car-hire office the woman behind the desk said in a casual manner, 'Have a good journey. Which way are you going?'

'Oh,' I replied, 'we're on a biblical tour and we want to spend a little time in Samaria because we want to see Mt Ebal and Mt Gerizim, where the tribes of Israel pronounced God's blessings and judgements.'

The woman's voice changed immediately: 'You are not taking one of our cars through Samaria; you'll get stoned!'

This took me totally by surprise. The land had been very peaceful during the time we were there a few days earlier (although we felt that the Israeli taxi driver had been a bit edgy when we visited the Tomb of the Patriarchs in Hebron) and there had been no trouble. Also in Jerusalem we had met a couple who had just driven south through Samaria without any problems (but then their car had had British number plates). However we had no option but to bypass Samaria and take the safe Jordan Valley route, then leave the car at the Capernaum office as planned.

We had some wonderful days at the Church of Scotland's guest house in Galilee, also visiting Nazareth and Megiddo. Next we took a bus to Haifa, and spent some days at what was then CMJ's Stella Carmel Guest House, very near to where Elijah had his dramatic confrontation with the prophets of Baal. Stella Carmel no longer exists, having been replaced by the beautiful Messianic congregation of Kehilat HaCarmel (Carmel Assembly). We were also able to spend a little time in the mainly Druze village of Isfiya and see just a little of Druze culture.

From there we went to the port city of Haifa itself, where we were welcomed by Canon Ronald and Laura Adeney who were exercising a greatly valued ministry in the land. We then spent a night at Beit Immanuel, the CMJ guest house in Jaffa, Tel Aviv. This wonderful, rambling, old house was once owned by Baron von Ustinov, Peter Ustinov's grandfather. The next day we flew home.

We found that conducting our own pilgrimage had advantages and disadvantages. On the plus side it felt very much like an exploration. We had to do our own digging, our own research; we were not just being fed information by experienced guides. Evaluating the evidence before us with Bibles in hand gave us the feeling we were making our own discoveries and enriching our understanding of long-known, well-loved biblical texts. On the negative side, as a small group of four, we were often trapped between two or more large groups who were being guided in different languages, which made it very difficult to think, let alone speak with each other. Also, as Elizabeth and I would find out when we went on subsequent organised tours, there was a lot we missed. But it was a memorable way of celebrating our silver and golden weddings, and it greatly enriched our already wonderful relationships.

CHAPTER 19

Unforeseen Developments

Being privileged with gifted leadership and ministry teams in our fellowship I was free to develop my own ministry in the wider Church. This, though I did not realise it at the time, was to prepare me for a future that was beyond anything I could have envisaged on my horizon. For some time I served on the national committee of the Eclectic Society. [1] For much of this time Revd John Stott was the chairman, and just being a member of his committee was a rich learning experience. I also joined the Fellowship of Parish Evangelism, which, as its name suggests, was set up to encourage church leaders to develop and hone good evangelistic gifts in their own ministries.

After a while the Church Pastoral Aid Society (CPAS), an organisation that was very closely involved in supporting parish ministry and church growth, began appointing clergy from growing churches, myself included, as regional evangelism advisors. The role involved visiting parishes that had requested help from CPAS in developing their evangelistic strategy. I was invited to cover an area of the West Midlands. After several consultations I discerned a disturbing underlying pattern linking many of the requests. These were instances where clergy who had exercised long and fruitful ministries in one parish were

---

[1] The Eclectic Society was first formed in the 18th century to encourage young evangelical clergy, then reformed by John Stott in the 1950s.

finding that for various reasons church life had plateaued and was even declining. In some cases, in response to their request for advice in developing a strategy for renewal and growth, the only honest advice I could give was that perhaps after their long, productive and often sacrificial service it was time to move on to pastures new and let someone with different gifts and a new vision develop the work in new directions. It was a difficult thing to say, but for them it was even more painful to hear. Many of these men (women had not yet been eligible for ordination) were now in their late fifties or early sixties and finding a new parish was not easy.

However what had up to now been a word for others soon stared me in the face. I had been at Bayston Hill for over 20 years. Two major building projects plus quite a lot of involvement in wider ministry projects had taken their toll, and now in my late fifties I had to ask myself whether my hard word to others was now a word for me. At my age it was now or never. I was already seeing the danger signs of plateauing and had to ask myself whether I had the vision and energy, or was I too deaf and too settled to hear God's call to move into new areas? The response came quickly and clearly from an unexpected direction.

Revd Jos Drummond, General Director of the CMJ, came to see me to ask me to consider applying for the recently vacated post of CMJ's Home Director. I had been a member of its governing council for many years but no thought of becoming a staff member had ever entered my mind. Was it for this that God had led me through that painful but very creative experience of re-entering my Jewish heritage? The next days were full of turmoil and mixed emotions. Should I apply? The opportunity of completing my ministry in such a post filled me with excitement, but also fear and awe: excitement about the possibilities that this post might bring to a Jewish believer in Jesus; fear as to whether I was really up to this task; and awe that God was giving me this opportunity in what would be the closing years of my full-time ministry. On the one hand the thought was almost like a 'new birth' experience; on the other hand the thought of leaving Christ Church was almost like a bereavement. And where would this leave Michael and Jane Tupper? Theirs had been an open-ended commitment to work with me as much as it had been to work in the parish. Wisely, from the beginning we had foreseen that such a situation might arise and we had at the time of their move already agreed that their coming should not preclude either of us moving to new pastures, should the call come. Nevertheless this situation was a real test of the depth of our commitment to one another.

Prayerfully I completed the necessary application forms and left it in the hands of my fellow CMJ council members as to whether this really was a call from God. Suffice it to say that there was no foregone decision and my interview by my fellow council members was intense and thorough. I was appointed, though, and a kind of confirmation of the rightness of this move and its timing was that it coincided with the completion of York House. We had finished the building side of the project; my successor would now have a clear hand, under Revd David Potter, Director of CCMH, in preparing for its day-to-day management.

The ensuing weeks and months were full of new challenges. Until now a house had always come with the job. CMJ provided accommodation for its area secretaries but not for its senior management team members, though it did have a shared equity provision. But there were difficulties to be overcome. First, house prices in St Albans, the location of CMJ's international HQ, were among the highest in England and at this point in the late 1980s were at their peak. Secondly the building society's reaction to someone not in the highest salary bracket asking for a first-time mortgage at the age of 57 brought reactions that are not easily forgotten! However all difficulties were overcome and we moved to St Albans in the first week of December 1988. Early the following year Elizabeth and I went to Israel on an orientation tour. This was very different from our previous family visit and underlined how quickly the land was developing. Our new life with CMJ brought with it some unexpected and at first unsettling feelings. It took me a long time to let go and accept that I no longer had pastoral responsibility for the people in our and the neighbouring streets. At first I felt guilty that I was not going out and knocking on their doors, and I was left wondering why no one was knocking on my door seeking to book a baptism or wedding, or to talk over some personal situation. Our home was now just our home and my office was half a mile away at CMJ HQ. But the demands and opportunities of the new job soon replaced these feelings.

Reporting to the governing council, which was responsible for developing the overall strategy of CMJ's work internationally, were three directors. These were the general director, who had oversight of the work internationally, the financial director and the home director (me), who had pastoral and developmental oversight of all the society's work in the UK.

My staff covered a huge spectrum of ministry. There was an education department, which ran the nationally renowned mobile Bible Come to Life Exhibition with a staff of three, which had been travelling the country for 100 years. There was the London outreach team, who presented faith in Jesus the Messiah – *Yeshua haMashiach* – in his original Jewish context, and at that time using a methodology based very much on that developed by Jews for Jesus working mainly in the United States. Also there was a group of six area secretaries covering the whole of the UK, who were responsible for maintaining links with supporting parishes and raising support for the work. Finally there was a home secretary, who was responsible for organising CMJ's annual conference and maintaining good links with past staff and supporters. This work was somewhat hidden, but invaluable in such a diverse context where individuals could so easily slip through the net.

As I began to plan my own aims and objectives in my new job, and to work out some priorities, I felt we needed some direct contact with the mainstream Jewish community and its leadership. I realised that almost inevitably there would be serious and understandable tensions, but I also saw that the deep misunderstandings that often led to public accusation could be better resolved by face-to-face discussions. When an 'anti-missionary' meeting at St John's Wood Synagogue was publicised I decided to attend in order to try to better understand some of the tensions underlying the often very public antagonisms. During the question time following two very strongly anti-missionary addresses, one by a rabbi and one by a West London vicar, I caught the chairman's eye and introduced myself as a Jewish believer in *Yeshua*/Jesus and one of these missionaries everyone was complaining about. I asked, 'Could we not think together about the central question "Who is Jesus?" If he is the Messiah then we all need to take him seriously, but if he is not then we could all forget about him. This question should form the foundation of ongoing discussion rather than public acrimony.' However the chairman swiftly closed this line of approach with a firm 'Next question, please.' Nevertheless, after the public part of the meeting concluded, I was able to talk with a well-respected rabbi whose background, though much more painful, had some parallel with mine. Another rabbi came to me and asked, 'What does it feel like to have made the one positive statement of the evening, only to be ignored by the chairman?' We shared some valuable and cordial correspondence for some time. Eventually, and for various reasons, both correspondences faded out, but it gave me sufficient hope that this might eventually become a way forward. At this time I made contact with the Council of Christians and Jews (CCJ) where I thought some opportunity of dialogue might be forthcoming. However the leadership made it clear that as long as I insisted in describing myself as a Messianic Jew or a Jewish believer in Jesus I was not eligible for membership. The reason given was that CCJ existed to foster dialogue between the two faiths, and those believers in Jesus who continued to describe themselves as Jews were a threat to the integrity of the dialogue. I found others who were in the same position and even Bishop Hugh Montefiore, formerly Bishop of Birmingham, with whom I had had several conversations, told me he had had his membership application returned. I recognised that CCJ was doing valuable and necessary work in overcoming deep misunderstandings and healing hurts between the two faiths, but felt that the preconditions set for membership greatly reduced the value of true and open dialogue. In fairness I want to say that things have changed – I am now a full and welcomed CCJ member – but I still regret that a forum for free and open discussion about Jesus is still very low on any agenda.

The value of making every effort to build relationships on the basis of finding common ground, and making every effort to avoid confrontation, was reinforced to me in a very dramatic and unexpected way when our team was working with a North London church as part of its regular outreach. I had begun a conversation with a Jewish man as he was working in his garden that was rapidly generating more heat than light. We then became aware of a sound in the sky that we both immediately recognised, as the Battle of Britain Memorial Flight, including the Lancaster, Spitfire and Hurricane, made a very low-level pass almost overhead. It quickly transpired that we had both worked on Lancasters in our time in the RAF some 40 years before, and this created a common bond between us. The whole tenor of our conversation changed. We still strongly differed as regards the basis of our faith, but a new respect and even cordiality had entered into our conversation.

In our time with CMJ Elizabeth and I were able to visit Israel twice, first on the brief orientation tour mentioned earlier, and then for three weeks when I was locum vicar of Christ Church, Jerusalem, while the vicar was on holiday in the UK. On both visits we were able to spend time in the Children's Memorial in Yad Vashem, which commemorates the one and a half million children who died in the Holocaust. As we listened to the names of the children being read out on an endlessly looping tape – which took several days to go round – I realised that had my journey from Czechoslovakia been delayed by only about five weeks, my name would have been on that tape! It was a very dramatic experience, but in a strange way, in a very tense and sometimes very aggressive city, that memorial is where I can find most peace.

One of the first things I did after returning to my office at CMJ HQ was to change the title of my job. No longer could I describe myself as CMJ's Home Director; that title rightly belonged to the leader of the work in Israel. I now described myself as UK Field Director. Despite my official title I was able to enjoy several overseas visits, and Elizabeth was sometimes able to travel with me.

In September 1994 I visited Helsinki in Finland at the invitation of a Lutheran group as the main speaker at their annual conference. I gave four talks entitled 'I found the Messiah', 'Messianic Jews: a Challenge to the Synagogue', 'Messianic Jews: a Challenge to the Church' and 'Messianic Jews: a Challenge to the world'. On arrival I found that my book, *Messianic Jews: Challenging Church and Synagogue*, which I had only written the previous year, had already been translated into Finnish and produced in a very attractive hardback format; and this was the first I had known about it! Speaking at this conference was a very challenging experience, not only because there were some very well-qualified theologians in the audience, but also because the talks were being filmed and there were several camera trolleys zooming around me on the podium! With the advantage of hindsight I realise that the titles of my talks were somewhat overblown, as was the title of my book, but these were the early, heady days of the Messianic Jewish movement, and perhaps looking at where we are now should be a lesson in humility.

After the conference I took a train to St Petersburg in Russia to spend a few days with a friend who had been a member of our Messianic fellowship in London, and was now teaching in some of the Messianic Jewish congregations there. What an eye-opener that was!

In May and June of 1996, Revd Janette Ross, the CMJ representative in Johannesburg, and Dougie St Clair-Laing, the representative in Cape Town, arranged for Elizabeth and me to undertake a six-week CMJ ministry tour of the work in South Africa. We flew to Johannesburg where I had several days of speaking and preaching engagements. At a picnic lunch following a Sunday service at which I had shared something of my story and spoken on Jewish and Gentile reconciliation through Jesus, the prince of peace, a man introduced himself to me. He rather hesitantly confessed that he had spent the war years as a member of the Hitler Youth. This was not the first time, nor would it be the last, that I had been challenged to practice what I had just preached! Another time I was very privileged to be invited to give a lecture in the Dutch Reformed University in Pretoria, where looking at the New Testament from the viewpoint of its Jewish roots was something of a new and not uncontroversial area! Yet another day was spent with one of the leaders in Alexandra township, where so many were still living in unutterably horrendous conditions, yet with great dignity and patience.

Janette then took us to Kruger National Park for a couple of days before driving us to our next engagement at a Bible college at White River for several days of teaching. While at White River we visited another Bible college, right up in the mountains, where pastors, mainly from small and remote churches from many parts of Africa, were receiving further training. These men possessed very little of this world's goods, but what really marked them out was their unquestionable faith and irrepressible joy. Out of their simple and yet profound Bible knowledge they had a natural affinity with anything Jewish, and any mention of Israel would be met by enthusiastic responses of 'Hallelujah!'

After this we flew down to Cape Town where Dougie and Hilda St Clair-Laing had arranged an intense and varied week of teaching and preaching in many different settings, as well as a wonderful week of holiday on the Cape Coast, for which someone lent us their beach bungalow and someone else lent us a car. Throughout our stay in South Africa we were overwhelmed with people's generosity.

While in Cape Town we had the joy of spending time with my foster brother, John Cumpsty, whom we had not seen for about 20 years. John and his family had emigrated so that he could take up the post of Director of Religious Studies at Cape Town University. Like me, John had begun as an engineer, but on hearing that I was withdrawing from my career in order to be ordained, he admitted that this was a calling he had been fighting for several years, and he likewise left engineering to be ordained. Remarkably John's father, Les, my foster father, on his retirement from an engineering career was also ordained, as I mentioned in an earlier chapter. So in the family we had three engineers becoming Christian ministers.

Following our time in Cape Town, Dougie and Hilda bade us farewell and we took a coach through the renowned and very beautiful Garden Route to Port Elizabeth. With Janette Ross again our guide and mentor, we undertook several speaking engagements here and in East London, as we worked our way up to Durban. In Durban I had a remarkable experience in what I would describe as a High Anglican church. The vicar was away at the time so it had been arranged that I would celebrate the Eucharist as well as preach. As we were preparing in the vestry before the service it became clear that I was not used to robing in traditional High Church vestments, so the churchwardens kindly suggested that I might be more comfortable wearing my *tallit* (Jewish prayer shawl) instead! This I did and it created a natural illustration for my sermon on the Jewish roots of the Christian faith, and the link between Passover and the Eucharist. From Durban, Janette drove us to Pietermaritzburg, where I had been invited for several days of teaching at African Enterprise, a well-known Bible College. African Enterprise had been founded in 1962 by the internationally accredited speaker and evangelist Michael Cassidy. Among many other initiatives, Michael had been involved in behind-the-scenes movements that brought together a wide spectrum of political leadership in dialogue in South Africa. His work has been widely acknowledged as an important contribution to the remarkably peaceful South African elections in April 1994. In 1996, at the request of President Nelson Mandela, he and other church leaders were deeply involved in spearheading Project Ukuthula, a very fruitful peace initiative in KwaZulu-Natal prior to the province's local government elections. On the first morning I was to speak briefly at an early-morning staff prayer meeting. I do not recall just how it happened, but Michael got out the message that all morning lectures were cancelled and the staff and I continued in lively discussion and prayer until lunchtime! After this Janette again bade us farewell, having arranged a hire car for us and a week's holiday in an African roundhouse in the Drakensburg Mountains. We then drove back to Johannesburg for our flight home. For the record, in the course of four weeks of ministry and two weeks of holiday, we had travelled 3000 miles within South Africa and I had spoken 43 times in churches or at other meetings.

1996 was a busy year for overseas travel and in October the Lausanne Consultation for Jewish Evangelism (part of the Lausanne Consultation for World Evangelism) invited me to present the keynote lecture at the European section meeting in Stuttgart, Germany. The title given to me was Post-*Sho'ah*[2] *Witness*. My purpose was to reflect on how the *Sho'ah* affected the way the Church's Jewish mission agencies understood their ministry. The conference committee decided that the inaugural talk should be open to the public. The Consultation usually used English as the agreed language for its meetings, but as this was to be public it was decided to provide facilities for simultaneous translation. Headphones were rented for all visitors, but just before the meeting began it was realised that none of the headphones had batteries in. We therefore had to fall back on sequential translation, which meant that the meeting would be much longer than planned or I would have to seriously shorten my talk. Fortunately I had two copies of my text, one of which I gave to the translator so that she could keep in step with me, as I would speak fairly quickly, so all went well.

---

[2] *Sho'ah* is Hebrew for 'desolation', and a term preferred by many to *Holocaust*. In the Bible *Holocaust* refers to the total burnt offering voluntarily offered as a sacrifice of love and praise to God. The deaths in the concentration camps were not a voluntary offering of praise.

While I was thoroughly enjoying my work with CMJ there was one aspect of the ministry that I and the other directors were finding very difficult. CMJ, together with many other church ministries, was going through a time of financial difficulty and we were having to make a number of our UK staff redundant. We eventually reached the point where any further reductions would mean closing one of the UK departments and making one of our younger staff redundant. However we urgently needed to save 50 per cent of a salary. The right course of action stared me in the face. With such a reduced staff the oversight of the UK ministry could be transferred to the general director, and as I only had two years to go before retirement it was obvious that I should bite the bullet and make myself redundant! There were, however, areas where I could still have important input into the work, so we created the post of Self-Employed Advisor and I worked for CMJ on an hourly basis as and when needed.

This not only gave CMJ the opportunity to reorganise its finances; it also helped with some changes in our home situation. For some years Elizabeth's mother's health had been failing. In the summer of 1992 Elizabeth and I moved to another house in St Albans, which had an attached flat where her parents could come and live semi-independently. On Easter Sunday 1995 Elizabeth's mother died peacefully at home, with family around her, just after we had shared in a short celebration of Jesus' wonderful resurrection.

By 1997 the amount of care Elizabeth's father needed had greatly increased so my early retirement made it possible for me to become more involved in supporting him. But there lay ahead things that we could not have foreseen.

CHAPTER 20

Now is the Time

It's 1991 and Elizabeth and I can put it off no longer; the momentous decision is made. We, together with my brother Arthur and his wife, Edith, are going to renew our childhood memories. We had previously suggested to Arthur that we would like to go, hoping that he and his wife would also want to come, but Arthur had not been keen, so Elizabeth and I had decided to go alone. However once we had made that decision Arthur could not bear to let us go without him.

It wasn't easy to find a common slot in our busy timetables, so Elizabeth and I booked a coach holiday and spent a week in Brno in the Czech Republic while Arthur and Edith were at a conference in Switzerland. Arthur and Edith then drove to meet us in Bratislava in Slovakia, and we all went up to Opava in the Czech Republic, where we spent a short time. The next day we drove to Vitkov, where my brother and I had lived as children, not knowing how much we would find and how we would feel. So much had changed that we decided not to go straight to our house, realising how great our disappointment would be if it was no longer there. Instead we drove to a high point from where either our hopes or our fears would be confirmed. Having arrived at the vantage point our purposes were dashed by a high-rise apartment block impeding our view, so we had no option but to

drive directly to where the house should be. And there it was, our beautiful house, looking somewhat uncared for, but definitely what we had so fervently hoped for. But what next? Should we just knock on the door? We didn't speak Czech. How would we explain ourselves? Fortunately we saw a man by the front gate so we were able to show him a photo of ourselves as children by our garden fence, taken just by the place where we were now standing. He immediately comprehended the situation and very warmly beckoned us in. He took us down to his garden shed and asked his wife, who was Turkish, to make us tea. Afterwards he was able to explain, with very few words and many hand gestures, that the house was now divided into four apartments. He showed us round his own part, and it seemed all so familiar – just as we had left it.

We then drove to the railway station. It was just as it had been all those years ago, when our parents had put us on a train and said goodbye. It seemed that I could almost feel the square paving slab on the platform where our goodbyes had been said. We said very little but our emotions were so strong that we did not want to linger too long. Instead we drove to a nearby stretch of forest where we used to go mushrooming, and true to form we soon found some beautiful ceps, which Arthur would take home and dry. We returned to Opava somewhat drained but very happy!

While in Opava, Elizabeth and I arranged to see a Czech pastor whose friend I had met on a visit to All Nations Christian

Vitkov railway station revisited.

College in Ware, Hertfordshire. Having introduced ourselves I was concerned that we were being given a rather cool and distant welcome. As we talked it soon became clear that I was the first Jewish person he had met. His only knowledge of Jews was that we had been the cause of his family's suffering because they had hidden some Jews during the war. As we talked further Elizabeth and I began to realise just how severe and how long the suffering of the Czech people had been, first under Nazi occupation and then under one of the most hardline Communist regimes that any European country had experienced.

The next day all four of us drove on to Prague, as tourists rather than pilgrims for it was a city we were unfamiliar with. The plan was to rest before our next challenge: a visit to our home city of Dresden.

When we got to Dresden's historic centre we could hardly believe our eyes. There was so little sign of damage; it was as beautiful as when we had left it. There was the wonderful Semperoper Opera House and the Dresden Porcelain Museum and the Swinger Centre in all their glory. Then we saw the stonemasons at work and realised that all these buildings had been painstakingly restored, stone by stone, according to their original plans. Only the Frauenkirche was left as a burnt-out shell – intended as a lasting memorial to the wartime destruction. Now, though, there has been a change of heart and this beautiful church has also been restored.

Our apartment block in Dresden.

Next came the emotional challenge of finding out what had happened to our home. First we drove past the dreary, grey concrete Communist buildings that marked the old inner suburbs, which had replaced those destroyed by the 1945 firestorm. Finally we came to the Gruna district and found Hehnahtstrasse 15, our old apartment! The whole area was like a time capsule; nothing had changed. Even the little corner shop was still at the end of the road. Well, actually there was one small change – our old apartment now sported a satellite TV dish! We could have left it yesterday, not half a century ago. We walked a couple of streets further and there was our school, in beautiful condition, but the same old school. Somehow this little area had escaped the destruction. Well satisfied by what we had seen, we spent a little more time in the city and then returned to the UK, visiting Bonn and Cologne on the way.

The following year our children wanted to explore their paternal roots and see at least the Czech part of my story. By now they were well scattered and had busy lives. Peter was married, and he and his wife Julie had a baby. We managed the trip by all travelling independently, then meeting up in Prague for a couple of days before driving to Vitkov to see the old house. Elizabeth and I had often talked with the children about my past, but this first-hand experience brought a new realism. Our children then again went their separate ways, but it had been a wonderful time of family togetherness for us all.

Our school in Dresden.

Elizabeth and I had something on our minds to resolve while we were in the Czech Republic: I had not got a birth certificate. So far on all my form fillings I had put a remembered date, but wondered if I would one day have to prove it – especially when it came to pension time! We found the registry office in Opava and explained what I wanted. Two ladies searched through two old record books but drew a blank. Eventually one asked me, 'Are you Protestant or Catholic?'

'Neither,' I replied. 'I'm Jewish.'

'Oh, you'll have to go to Prague, to the Jewish Registry Office,' came the reply. 'All the Jewish records are kept separately.'

'Give us a couple of days; we'll have to go down to the vaults,' said the lady in the Jewish Registry. So the following Monday

Re-visiting the sandpit in Dresden.

morning we returned and were duly presented with a copy of my birth certificate – and they wouldn't even accept payment for it!

A couple of years later the leaders of our old church in Bayston Hill wanted me to make a twinning arrangement with a Czech church, so Elizabeth and I, together with Michael and Jane Tupper, sallied forth. First we went to Dresden, to our old flat. Jane persuaded me to be bolder this time, so we went round the back to where the sandpit was and I sat in the place where, in 1935, I had first been called a 'dirty Jew', and so many memories came flooding back. I also rang the doorbell on number 15; a lady came to the window but we did not have sufficient language in common to communicate properly. I tried to explain I had

Speaking with the present occupant of our apartment.

lived there once but I think she thought I was trying to reclaim the apartment, so closed the window. I decided to leave it there. We then went to a small town about 30km from Prague where we made the twinning and where Michael was able to speak through an interpreter. We learnt that a Russian tank detachment had been based in the town during the Communist years and many of the congregation had experienced great suffering. We then drove to Vitkov to show Michael and Jane the house where I had lived and outside there was a pile of builder's rubble. I noticed an old but unbroken quarry tile from our kitchen floor, which I put in the boot of our car and brought home. It is now a treasured part of my memories.

Even after these visits I still did not feel all had been put to rest, so in 2006 Elizabeth and I flew to Krakow, Poland, and on Wednesday 20 September we visited Auschwitz. I had no idea of how I was going to react when the day of the visit finally came. I was fearful but I knew it had to be done. Fortunately we had a few days in Krakow before the actual visit, and in a way this helped me to 'acclimatise'. Also on the coach journey from our hotel to the camp there was an excellent video to prepare visitors. What I was not prepared for was the sheer number of visitors: right through our time there we were shoulder to shoulder; a small part of a huge crowd. Yet even with such numbers what was surprising was the utter silence of the place. In these circumstances I found it quite difficult to get in touch with my immediate emotions. In as far as I had been able to prepare myself I had imagined Elizabeth and myself having space to be alone; with all these people I felt myself to be one more observer of the enormity of the terrible things we were all seeing. Only afterwards, when we got back to our hotel, when we could be alone, could I allow my deeper feelings to surface. I didn't know what to expect but I was overwhelmed with a sense of peace, a sense of healing, a sense of wholeness in that the final closed and dark room in my past life had been opened and there was nothing to fear. Over the years that have elapsed since these feelings have not left me.

Our guide at Auschwitz was a very compassionate young woman, probably only in her mid-twenties. How she managed to guide so sensitively day after day I cannot imagine. After the tour she even helped me with some family research. Next we visited a friend in Opava who had arranged for Elizabeth and I to meet the Mayor of Vitkov. Then, after more family research in Prague, we flew home. Now I feel I have probably done as much research as I can and feel at peace.

CHAPTER 21

Constant Change is Here to Stay

Returning our thoughts to life in the UK, I had become involved in The Centre for Biblical and Hebraic Studies, which had been formed in 1995 under the leadership of David Forbes. The focus of this centre was to study and teach the background of the biblical intertestamental period as the basis for better understanding the life and teaching of Jesus and the formation of the Church. The shorter name for this centre was Pardes, an acronym of *peshat, remez, derash* and *sod,* four ways of interpreting and understanding the Hebrew Bible. [3] Pardes was part of the wider work of Prophetic Word Ministries (PWM), founded by Dr Clifford Hill, which was in the process of moving to new premises in Moggerhanger near Bedford. Clifford had invited me to become a member of the *Pardes* support team.

Sadly, in March 1997, David died, so Clifford convened a meeting of the support team to plan for the future of the work and seek out a new director. The meeting was planned for the day after I was due to return from the International Messianic Jewish Conference in Puerto Vallarta, Mexico, but as it happened

---

[3] Peshat (פְּשָׁט) — "plain" ("simple") or the direct meaning.
Remez (רֶמֶז) — "hints" or the deep (allegoric: hidden or symbolic) meaning beyond just the literal sense.
Derash (דְּרַשׁ) — from Hebrew darash: "inquire" ("seek") — the comparative (midrashic) meaning, as given through similar occurrences.
Sod (סֹד) — (pronounced with a long O as in 'bone') — "secret" ("mystery") or the mystical meaning, as given through inspiration or revelation

our stay there was delayed by a day so when we arrived back at Gatwick a car was waiting to rush me up to Moggerhanger. The conference had been very demanding, with some long discussions and big decisions to make. On top of that the flight home had been very tiring because of faults in the aircraft's air-conditioning system. So I was not prepared for what was awaiting me. I had thought we would be deciding who might take on the leadership of this ministry. But as soon as the meeting started it became clear that during my absence the decision had already been taken that I should fill the post! And it also became clear that a fairly quick answer was expected! Was my retirement really going to be put on ice? How would this affect the plans Elizabeth and I had made? Given the circumstances of David Forbes' untimely death, and that Pardes was just then fulfilling a real role in New Testament teaching, I offered to take on the leadership for twelve months, to give time for a younger long-term leader to be found. However, Clifford wanted a three-year minimum commitment, so in the end we agreed on a part-time three-year contract, with flexi-time and the opportunity to work from home when this was possible. This fitted in well with the family commitments I had made.

I hit the ground running fast. There was much to catch up on, both in terms of leading programmes that had already been prepared, and in building relationships, especially with those involved in the Jerusalem School of Synoptic Studies, which was based mainly in Jerusalem and the United States. I was of course familiar with much of the work of those involved but personally had had little contact with any of them. The very varied work of the Centre included publishing the Pardes quarterly magazine, organising regular day-long study conferences and developing distance-learning programmes.

Amid this regular work came one of my most enjoyable and fulfilling challenges: the production of a book that was to be a fitting tribute to the ministry of David Forbes. I was to be Managing Editor and we appointed an editorial team. We titled the book *Roots and Branches: Explorations into the Jewish Context of the Christian Faith.* As we discussed the contents and format it naturally fell into three parts: 'Jesus in His Hebraic Setting', 'The Developing Faith' and 'The Growing Tree'. Each part would comprise three essays, some written by internationally recognised scholars and some by members of our own staff. I was to contribute one called 'From Jesus to Paul'. The whole work was to be prepared and published in-house. As well as chairing regular meetings of the editorial and publishing team I maintained long and detailed correspondence with contributors from Israel and the United States. It was a monumental task, which we completed in less than one year, and it was truly a fitting tribute to David Forbes.

In 1998 I had the pleasure of leading a PWM Israel tour together with Jenny Forbes, David's widow, who was a tower of strength throughout my time with Pardes. This was my fourth visit to Israel and I was amazed how much it had changed since my last visit. In particular, the Messianic congregations were growing fast and developing deep fellowship links with some of the Palestinian Arab congregations in the land.

In August 2000 I was invited back to Finland for three weeks, and this time Elizabeth was also invited to come with me. My first visit had been at the invitation of the Finnish Lutheran Church, but this time the invitation came from two ministries involved in the study of Jewish roots, Gesher and Shoreshim. The first week was spent in Helsinki, where a very varied programme had been prepared. We shared in a *Shabbat* meal on the second day, and attended a synagogue service on the morning of the third. In the afternoon I preached at a special service of the International Evangelical Church, which took place in the well-known and dramatic building known as the Helsinki Rock Church. There were other meetings in the week, but we were also able to see the beautiful sights of Helsinki and sample some of the fish delicacies from the harbour food stalls. We were also able to visit the composer Jean Sibelius's house. The following weekend I spoke at the Gesher Conference at Heinola, together with Risto Santala, a well-known and respected Finnish theologian. I was also invited to preach at the Lutheran Parish Church in Heinola. We were then lent a typical Finnish lakeside timber cottage for a few days, and a car to go with it. Here we immensely enjoyed the mandatory Finnish sauna, but we chickened out of the traditional plunge into the very cold lake afterwards.

To complete our time in Finland we were taken to a very large lodge in the middle of the forest near to the Russian border. There a group of Christians welcomed Jews, mainly from Moscow, either for a short holiday or to prepare them for *aliah* ('going up') – that is, emigrating to Israel. For a few days they were given good meals and access to doctors and dentists, who gave their time freely for all necessary treatment. There again I was invited to speak, and not only were my words translated into Finnish, but then from Finnish into Russian. That was one of the most challenging talks I have ever given, as several times the Russian translator asked the Finnish translator to ask me to repeat what I had just said – which I had by then almost forgotten – making it quite difficult to maintain the thread of my thoughts. It was an extempore talk in the first place and I have often wondered how it came out in the final Russian version.

By now Elizabeth's father's health had deteriorated so much that he had to go into full-time care. This meant we needed to downsize considerably and, as my work with Pardes would soon be coming to an end, we decided that this was a good time to move to a less busy place. We were greatly attracted to Thame, a lovely market town in Oxfordshire with a very lively church, and when a bungalow 'ripe for renovation' came on the market we made our move.

CHAPTER 22

Justice Issues

In my time at Pardes I became particularly interested in justice issues. It was becoming clear that crime was on the increase in many parts of the UK; the prison population was growing, reoffending by released prisoners was on the increase and a new approach to law and order, crime and punishment, was urgently needed. Where might we find a new approach to this whole matter? What were the principles on which our present judicial system was founded? What light might the Bible shed on this subject? I had friends who had studied law and qualified as barristers. Looking at the areas they had covered I came to realise that much of their study, and much of our legal system, was heavily based on Roman law. Of course it is recognised that the Roman Empire was one of the great civilising influences on world history, and many of the principles it developed are still applied in today's society. Yet the Bible, including the Hebrew Bible, had had an enormous influence in the formation of our national culture. One passage from the Hebrew Bible particularly attracted my attention because it epitomised for me a whole new way of looking at justice issues:

The LORD *said to Moses: 'If anyone sins and is unfaithful to the* LORD *by deceiving a neighbour about something entrusted to them or left in their care or about something stolen, or if they cheat their neighbour, or if they find lost property and lie about it, or if they swear falsely about any such sin that people may commit – when they sin in any of these ways and realise their guilt, they must return what they have stolen or taken by extortion, or what was entrusted to them, or the lost property they found, or whatever it was they swore falsely about. They must make restitution in full, add a fifth of the value to it and give it all to the owner on the day they present their guilt offering. And as a penalty they must bring to the priest, that is, to the* LORD, *their guilt offering, a ram from the flock, one without defect and of the proper value. In this way the priest will make atonement for them before the* LORD, *and they will be forgiven for any of the things they did that made them guilty.'*

Leviticus 6:1–7

Laying aside the detail we can see a principle that the first response to a crime must be that the offender, as far as possible, makes personal restitution to his victim. Only after this can broader issues be dealt with. Is there something here that can be applied in our secular situation? I suggest the following: in any criminal resolution the victim must be involved from the beginning, and restitution for his or her loss or hurts should be the primary concern. Only then should any further action be decided on.

This is a far cry from our current criminal justice system, which is based on Crown versus the accused, with the victim and his or her losses and feelings being kept at a distance until as late as possible in the proceedings. Things have changed and are changing, and more recently victims have been allowed to express their own feelings to the court before sentences are passed, but even now any compensation for the victim's losses or hurts are paid out from a criminal compensation fund rather than directly by the perpetrator. Why the difference? The basis of the English legal system on the Roman model means the emphasis is on objectivity, on making the punishment fit the crime, whereas the Hebraic pattern has its main emphasis on restoration. In the latter the *offender* restores the victim's situation as far as possible to where it was before the crime was committed and, where possible, thereby restoring or creating a relationship between victim and perpetrator. In technical terms, the British legal system is based on a contractual relationship between the citizen and the state, whereas the Hebraic pattern is based on a covenantal relationship for all its people.

Thus far I had not shared my thinking with anyone outside the circle of Pardes, nor had the whole concept of restorative justice had much public exposure. So it came as a complete surprise when I received an invitation to join the Oxfordshire Youth

Offending Service, which was trialling restorative justice. My personal preference would have been to work with adult rather than youth offenders, but the scheme was not at that time being trialled among adults in Oxford, so with some trepidation but also a sense of excitement I accepted the invitation. The kinds of cases we would handle would be limited to break-ins, vandalism and minor gang skirmishes, not major crimes, but these were just the sort the traditional justice system found difficult to resolve. Our training was intense and included some challenging role-plays that helped us to get into the mindset of both victim and offender. The ultimate challenge was how we might set up and oversee a face-to-face meeting between the two parties in a constructive way. Our young offenders could not see beyond the immediate material effects of the things stolen or the damage done. They had no concept of the personal and psychological hurt they had inflicted upon their victims, who were often left fearful and withdrawn from wider society. And in the minds of the victims there often grew up a picture of the offender of almost demonic proportions, which bore little resemblance to the youngsters themselves.

I worked with the Young Offenders Service for about two years, and during this time I was challenged in many ways and had to revise many of my presuppositions. That many (most?) of the young people we were dealing with came from single-parent families is well documented, though it was not politically correct to dwell on that. There was good reason for this: it is all too easy to develop a somewhat negative attitude towards single parents, and this is where I was most challenged. After involvement in only a very few cases I developed a real respect for most of these single parents (mainly mums). Most of them were single through no fault of their own; most of them had been abandoned by the men in their lives and were struggling against all odds to keep their families together and bring their children up to be good members of their community. But the odds were heavily stacked against them. Also in many cases they were not strictly single parents in that there were husbands and fathers at home. However, in reality, the menfolk did very little in terms of involving themselves in the care, nurture and development of their children. In fact their influence in some cases was negative. More than once I was ashamed of being a man!

Two things especially disappointed me. The first was that the vast majority of victims did not want to be involved in the restorative justice process. For various reasons they did not want to meet those who had caused them harm or damage, and this seriously negated what we were trying to achieve. However much we tried to explain the principles and possible benefits of what we were working on, there was an ingrained feeling on the part of most victims that this was a 'soft option' as far as the offender was concerned, and that any meeting with the offenders would be too painful and in the end counterproductive. In these instances the young offenders had to undertake some work in the community and therefore this was little different from the kinds of community sentences that could be handed out by the traditional youth courts. Secondly we were further limited because of insufficient resources for the trial to be really effective. There were not enough trained Youth Offending Service workers. Most of those I had the privilege to work with were well trained and very professional, but they had such large caseloads that they could not give sufficient quality time to the offenders and their families.

Nevertheless I enjoyed about two years of this work and the main reason I left had nothing to do with anything I have so far said. Almost all the young offenders we saw were astonishingly timid in the presence of the panel, however informal and unthreatening we tried to make our presence and our surroundings, and the result was that when they spoke their voices were often little more than whispers. All the bravado that had got them into their present situation seemed somehow to evaporate. In the circumstances my frequent need to ask them to repeat what they had said and to speak up was not conducive to a relaxed, open and creative discussion, so I decided that in the best interests of the work it was time I retired.

However my 'new' retirement was not to last long for, again without any initiative on my part, I was invited to become a volunteer chaplain with Thames Valley Police. 'Well, why not?'

I thought. At least in relating to policemen my hearing loss, which was not all that severe, should not be a problem! And the nature of the work would not be unrelated to what I had been doing, though I would see it very much from the other side. Instead of working with law-breakers I would now be working with law-enforcers. It felt a bit like 'if you can't beat them join them'. Our training was thorough and fascinating as we spent time with the various police departments, including the armed response units, the dog handlers and the motorway patrols. We were welcomed right through the force, from the Chief Constable to the officer on the beat. The force had its own welfare department, but sometimes police officers wanted to talk about any personal problems with someone who was completely outside the system, and yet well versed in what the work involved. However new developments required chaplains to undergo more of the physical side of police training, and the angina that I had developed about 15 years beforehand, though not getting worse, meant that I would have to resign from this fascinating and fulfilling ministry.

CHAPTER 23

Back to Basics

Quite unintentionally, but perhaps quite naturally, our move to Thame had taken me outside the sphere of Jewish life and maybe I needed a time of readjustment. But change was now coming from several directions and at a pace that was very hard to keep up with.

For a number of years Elizabeth and I had been on visits to Beth Shalom, the Holocaust Centre near Newark in Nottinghamshire, but our connection with the centre had not gone beyond visiting on their various open days. Gradually I got to know the leaders and staff, and was invited to join the team of people – some concentration camp survivors, others child refugees – who shared their stories with the many groups who visited. Over the course of time I have become a regular speaker and now visit once or twice a month.

As this new direction was developing someone let our local paper, the *Thame Gazette*, know something of my story and invitations to speak came in from a variety of local organisations. One of the most challenging came at very short notice from our local secondary school, Lord Williams's School. Every January, during Holocaust Memorial Week, the Holocaust Educational Trust had supplied a speaker to cover the subject for Year 9, for whom this subject was included in the National

Curriculum. In 2006 one of the visiting speakers had had to pull out at short notice and one of the staff, having seen my story in the local paper, asked me whether I could fill in. The outcome has been that I have been covering the whole week since then, and over the past eight years I have shared my story with about 2500 Year 9 students at this school alone. I have also had invitations from many other schools in many parts of the UK, and from a variety of other organisations, especially the University of the Third Age. More recently I have had the privilege of joining the Holocaust Education Trust panel of speakers, which has greatly increased the breadth of my schools involvement.

For Elizabeth and me August 2011 was one of the great milestones in our life as we had the great joy of celebrating our golden wedding. About sixty guests from our family and long friendship circles gathered for a wonderful meal and relaxing time for reminiscing and catching up with one another at the Thame Barns Centre. Sadly Roger Briggs, who fifty years previously had been my best man was unable to be there. After a lifelong ministry among the Inuit he was now settled in Canada but to our joyful surprise he had already arranged with the Barns Centre that at an appropriate moment he would phone us and we were able to link our conversation into the Barns PA system. That added so much to the joy of the day. Also we had the privilege of having Sir Nicholas Winton as a very special guest. One of the unexpected joys of our move to Thame is that we now live only 25 miles from Sir Nicholas Winton. Elizabeth and

At our Golden Wedding Party.

Our wonderful day.

With Sir Nicholas Winton.

Our lovely offspring: l to r David, Helen and Peter

I have been able to visit him fairly frequently, sharing deep friendship and visits to the local pub.

Over the past few years we have enjoyed a number of Kindertransport reunions, including our 75th anniversary in 2013. Their Royal Highnesses the Prince of Wales and the Duchess of Cornwall have generously held two receptions for us at Clarence House and St James's Palace. There has been a great deal of publicity in the media, and Sir Nicholas Winton has received many honours, especially in the Czech Republic. The Czech film director Matej Mináč has produced the film *Nicky's Family*, in which the lives of some of those rescued, and

With Sir Nicholas Winton in Prague.

the continuing influence of their families, is investigated and recorded. In 2011 Elizabeth and I had the great pleasure of attending the film's premiere in Prague.

More recently I have joined the CCJ, where some of issues that have divided our two communities are much more open to creative discussion than they have been in the past. We are living in a world where both Jewish and Christian communities are coming under increasing pressure and, in places, increasing persecution. I believe we can no longer afford either the luxury or the scandal of our continuing divisions and must work together to find and further develop our common ground.

Wanderings and Wonderings

Sunday February 28th 1988 is a date that I shall always remember. It had been a pretty ordinary Sunday and Elizabeth and I were well settled down for a quiet evening when the phone rang.

'Hello, John; it's Jane. Did you watch *That's Life!*?'

'No, Jane, not this evening. Why do you ask?'

'Well, you were on it.'

This book has come to birth after several years of gestation and labour. In many different ways I've been a Wandering as well as a Wondering Jew. What I have learnt and constantly had to relearn is that we can't just *watch* life; inevitably we are *on* the journey that we call life and on that journey we experience many changes. We can't choose our starting points and many of the changes are beyond our control.

However I have chosen the title of *A Wondering Jew* because, whatever external constraints there have been on my wanderings, my real journey has been a *wondering*; a spiritual journey on which my guide and companion has been the One who said, 'I am the true and living way.' [4] There have been

---

[4] In John 14:6 most Bible translations record Jesus as saying, 'I am the way, the truth and the life.' Despite my limited Greek knowledge I am assured that the Greek can be equally translated, 'I am the true and living way.' This, to me, is much more dynamic and Hebraic, and sits more comfortably with the experiences of those first believers, who were sometimes described as 'Followers of the Way' (Acts 9:2; 22:4)

many times when I have argued with my guide, when I have questioned his way, when I still need correction or reassurance, and when I have to admit that I don't know. I will recount two recent incidents.

During the question time after telling my story to a school group in Llandudno, a girl asked me, 'If you had been a non-Jewish boy in Germany in the 1930s, whose side might you have been on?' I know what I would have liked to have said, but I immediately knew this answer would have been too easy and glib. After a long silence I acknowledged that if I had been brought up in very different circumstances I could have been one of the blackshirts. I emphasised how important it is that we keep a close watch on the forces that mould and develop our thinking and actions; that we need to be aware of our own weak points where we all too easily follow the crowd. We need to develop our own sense of right and wrong that can withstand any adverse pressure to conform to the herd mentality which can so easily take over our lives. The situation in the question has thankfully not been part of my journey, and I must not be quick to judge those who have had to walk that way.

More recently I experienced something that I hesitate to call a vision, because that would be too grand a title and I'm not given to such exalted experiences. A vision includes a direct revelation and the deepening insight or application of some spiritual truth as it relates to a particular situation. I don't claim that for my experience. However what I do at least say is that it was a resolution at a deep, subconscious level of a conflict that had for some time been resolved only at a conscious level and was therefore, as far as I was aware, dealt with and finished. This is what happened.

Momentarily I was in heaven, and on looking round I saw a real wow of a party. Isn't that what heaven is all about? I went to see who was partying and there I saw my parents, grandparents and cousins, and all my lost family having a whale of a time together. And who else was with them? The Nazi leadership who had caused all their pain! Immediately my head went into cynical and critical overdrive. *'This can't be'* my mind protested, but my heart rejoiced. For a while my whole being went into a schizophrenic mind–heart battle, which my heart eventually won – so I joined the party! I accept that this was probably all at a psychological and not a theological level, but for me this does not in any way lessen its precious value. I'm not seeking to pronounce on the eternal destiny of the Nazi leadership; it is not for me to judge. But I am now reassured that the last vestiges of the sting of an unforgiving spirit have been withdrawn from my life, and I am at peace with those who have caused unutterable hurt. Yet the question remains: if I can imagine such a miracle could God do it? I don't know, but in the meantime I shall continue on my wonderings and wanderings with the peace and presence of my gracious and loving Companion and Guide.

Might not the greatest divine judgement be that the Nazis have to eternally live with and love the very people they once tried to destroy? That would be the ultimate divine reversal.

I wonder!

Farewell Letter from Our Parents

The following is a translation of the final letter from our parents, Curt and Trude Feige, which they wrote shortly before their internment in Auschwitz.

Arthur and I received this letter shortly after the end of the war, but I have left it until this point in the book because it had been tragically lost. Though I remember its arrival I had forgotten the detail and wonder of its contents. It was only found recently by my brother's children, when sorting through his effects after his death, and so its sheer power and love have only latterly impacted my life, as they continue to do every time I read it.

From Mother

Dear Boys
When you receive this letter the war will be over because our friendly messenger won't be able to send it earlier. We want to say farewell to you who were our dearest possession in the world, and only for a short time were we able to keep you.

Fate has not left us for months now. In Jan. 1942 the Weilers were taken; we still don't know where to and whether they are still alive. In June Grandmother Betty, in Sept. Aunt Marion, Uncle Willi and Pauli, in Oct. your Steiner grandparents, in Nov. your 90-year-

old Great-Grandmother and the Bermans. In Dec. it will be our turn and the time has therefore come for us to turn to you again and to ask you to become good men and think of the years we were happy together. We are going into the unknown; not a word is to be heard from those already taken.

Thank the Cumpstys who have kept you from a similar fate. You took of course a piece of your poor parents' hearts with you when we decided to give you away. Give our thanks and gratitude to all who are good to you.

From Father

Your dear mother has told you about the hard fate of all our loved ones. We too will not be spared and will go bravely into the unknown with the hope that we shall yet see you again when God wills. Don't forget us and be good.

I too thank all the good people who have accepted you so nobly.

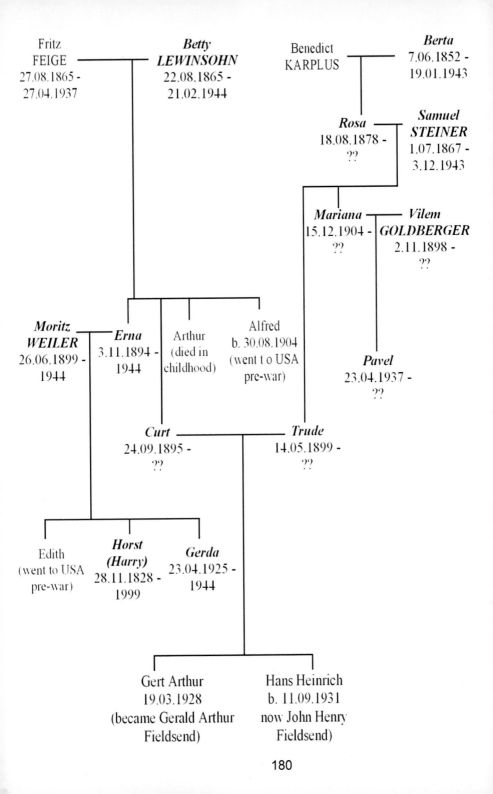

Fritz
FEIGE
27.08.1865 -
27.04.1937

Betty
LEWINSOHN
22.08.1865 -
21.02.1944

Benedict
KARPLUS

Berta
7.06.1852 -
19.01.1943

Rosa
18.08.1878 -
??

Samuel
STEINER
1.07.1867 -
3.12.1943

Mariana
15.12.1904 -
??

Vilem
GOLDBERGER
2.11.1898 -
??

Moritz
WEILER
26.06.1899 -
1944

Erna
3.11.1894 -
1944

Arthur
(died in
childhood)

Alfred
b. 30.08.1904
(went to USA
pre-war)

Pavel
23.04.1937 -
??

Curt
24.09.1895 -
??

Trude
14.05.1899 -
??

Edith
(went to USA
pre-war)

Horst
(Harry)
28.11.1828 -
1999

Gerda
23.04.1925 -
1944

Gert Arthur
19.03.1928
(became Gerald Arthur
Fieldsend)

Hans Heinrich
b. 11.09.1931
now John Henry
Fieldsend)

NOTES

Curt and Trude Feige
Interned in Auschwitz Concentration Camp 26.2.1943, date of death unknown.

Betty Feige (nee Lewinsohn)
Interned Terezin (Teresienstadt) Concentration Camp 14.7.1942 and died there on 21.2.1944

Berta Karplus
Interned Terezin Concentration Camp 18.11.1942, died there on 19.01.1943

Samuel Steiner
Interned Terezin Concentration Camp on 24.10.1942, died there on 03.12.1943

Rosa Steiner
Interned Terezin 24.10.1942; transferred to Auschwitz Concentration Camp 18.05.1944, date of death unknown.

Mariana Goldberger (nee Steiner)
Interned Terezin 08.09.1942; transferred to Auschwitz Concentration Camp 26.01.1943, date of death unknown

Vilem Goldberger
Interned Terezin 08.09.1942; transferred to Auschwitz Concentration Camp 26.01.1943, date of death unknown

Pavel Goldberger
Interned Terezin 08.09.1942; transferred to Auschwitz Concentration Camp 26.01.1943, date of death unknown

Moritz Weiler
Died in Riga Stutthof Concentration Camp, Riga, 1944

Erna Weiler (nee Feige)
Died in Riga Stutthof Concentration Camp, Riga, 1944.

Gerda Weiler
Died in Riga Stutthof Concentration Camp, Riga, 1944

Horst Weiler (Harry)
Interned in Bergen Belsen Concentration Camp, survived and died in Philadelphia in 1999.